THE WORKHOUSE

AND THE WEALD

Dorothy, aged 13.

THE WORKHOUSE AND THE WEALD

Dorothy Hatcher

Meresborough Books
1988

Published by Meresborough Books, 17 Station Road, Rainham, Kent. ME8 7RS

Meresborough Books is a specialist publisher of books about Kent (with a few on Sussex). A list of books currently available is at the back of the book.

ISBN 0948193 360

Printed by Whitstable Litho, Whitstable, Kent

CONTENTS

Chapter 1

THE WORKHOUSE

I shall always remember Fan, a little wizened old woman with a knot of black hair screwed into a bun at the back of her head. Fan looked after us in what was the nursery part of the old Tenterden workhouse. I am sure in her way she was fond of us, but had to obey orders to keep the children quiet and well behaved. There was a notice on the wall, which I found out afterwards laid out the rules for the children's ward. I found her way of caring for the young very different from what I did for my own children in later life.

Morning began with breakfast, porridge, bread and margarine. I do not remember much else about the other meals. Breakfast remained in my memory because of what followed directly the meal was over. Every small child was placed on a potty and had to stay there until it had performed, and woe betide the child who had nothing to show for the morning ritual – it meant a hard slap on the bottom and I was often the recipient of the punishment. Fan seemed to think everyone could oblige at will.

Meanwhile, the older children got ready for school. They were dressed all alike in brown dresses, black cloaks and round brown hats. Of course I do not remember all that from that time, but I saw them many times later on. In fact I cannot recollect much at all about that time in my life – I was just four.

One incident does stand out in my life though. One day I was taken by Fan along the corridor to see Matron, always an alarming occasion because it was the threat held over us for any misbehaviour. 'I shall take you along to see Matron' Fan said, so it was with some alarm that I went along with Fan that morning. She hadn't said a word about why we were going and of course I feared the worst. When we arrived however, Matron smiled and said 'Do you know what today is?' Of course I did not. 'It is your birthday' she said, and gave me a lovely doll. It had lovely curly hair and brown eyes. I had never had anything like it before. In fact I had never seen anything like it. I remember cuddling it to me as I stood in front of Matron as she continued what she had to say. 'You are now four years old' she said. 'Old enough to be "sent out".' Most of what she said went over my head, but I did know that people used to come to the door of the nursery and look at one or two children and a few days afterwards they would be taken to Matron's room and be seen no more.

Fan and I went back to the day room where she promptly took away my lovely doll and locked it in the cupboard, 'to keep it clean' she said. I never saw it again and later on I discovered it was used for each little girl in turn, the boys having a toy more suited to them. I do not recollect seeing my mother at all, but I must have done as the rule was that all 'inmates' should be allowed to see their children if they had any living at the house. Saturday was the day allowed for visits.

An ox-drover at work in Sussex.

One particular day Fan put on my clean pinny and I was taken to the door to be seen by a lady, but she chose the other girl and I was taken back into the nursery again. This went on quite a few times until one day I was taken to see a lady and gentleman. They stood at the door and Fan said 'We can't get a home for this one — she is so ugly.' Well, I never had any looks to write home about and it appears that at that time I was positively ugly. However, the lady and gentleman looked at both of us — there was another girl as well as myself — and straight away chose me. I then went up to Matron who said she was glad to have found a home for me at last.

I was given a set of clothes, two of everything, and a few days later I was collected by my new mother. I was told to be sure to be a good girl or she would be bringing me back again. I sat in a pushchair and was taken to their home at Smallhythe.

They told me later that they chose me because I looked all eyes and nose and was such a funny little thing. They were sure I was just what they needed to make their home a complete family.

I found out later that the couple had just got married. It was 1909. 'Auntie Bea' as I came to call her, had spent all her working life as a nurse, going into a home a month before a baby was expected and staying a month after it was born. I heard many tales of the lovely homes she had stayed in and, as the nurse, she was waited on by the staff of the house and did no housework herself. Consequently she became very untidy in her own home and always seemed to be in a muddle.

Working in the fields left time to make friends.

Uncle Ambrose was a much older man, at least thirty years older than his wife. It was really a marriage of convenience, for both needed companionship and neither would have dreamed of living together unless they were married, so that is what they did and decided to foster a child to make it a family.

I soon came to love this couple and they were, to me, my parents. Uncle was a rosy cheeked, bewhiskered old man, who had been an ox-drover in Sussex. Quiet and always gentle with me whatever I did, never once did he raise a hand to me and I know there were times when I deserved it. He would have made a lovely Father Christmas with his rosy cheeks and bushy beard.

Auntie Bea was much younger but still was quite old to take on the responsibility of looking after such a child as me. It couldn't have been easy for her. She made up for any shortcomings by her great love for me. As I grew older, I realised she was looked on by others as eccentric and this was certainly the case, but she showed me the first love I had ever known, a love which lasted a lifetime. Both stood by me through all that happened in later life – to me they were always my parents.

Chapter 2

MY MOTHER

Perhaps this is the time to tell you about my mother, Kate, and her family. I remember my grandmother, whose name was Emmeline, as a small woman with white hair always worn in a snood. About once a month I would come out of school to find her waiting for me at the end of the school lane. She would take me into a shop and let me buy sweets, then she would go on to see my mother who was still living in what was called 'The Union'.

For most of her life Grandmother had been looking after a man who had been left a widower with a family of small children. It appears that at that time, anyone left with young children to bring up could ask a neighbour to lend them a girl to housekeep for him. Sometimes the man would apply to the workhouse for a woman to be supplied, and this they would agree to do with the proviso that the man would do the right thing and marry the woman. Some did, but more often than not the poor woman would find after a few years, when the man's own children by the dead wife were old enough to carry on, that she would be turned out with her children by the man, and there would be nothing for her but to go back to the workhouse again. In the case of my grandmother, she stayed with the man as his housekeeper right until he died. She herself was a good age then, with three children, Kate – my mother – and two boys. Except for the wedding ring she was his wife, but when he died there was no provision made for her, and she ended her days in an infirmary.

My mother and her two brothers went to stay with Greatgran who was herself a widow. Every day mother would help in the house and then out in the fields working with the boys. From what my mother told me she worked from morning till night and then helped in the house while her brothers were out. This was quite common at that time. A girl was just a chattel. In mother's case, she had to work to pay for her keep. It was a dreadful thing that an illegitimate child carried a stigma all her life. It is only just beginning to be looked at in a different light. The pity of it was that mother had been given a good education, paid for by an aunt who sent her to a private school. The aunt was childless, it appears, and would have liked to take Kate to live with her, but mother was very useful to her grandmother, and at a very early age could do such things as thistle spudding, chopping firewood, filling the copper and so on.

Every Monday was washday, and early in the morning there would be faggots to get in, made by her brothers in the winter and tied up by mother with a pliable thong. (There is a knack in doing this and I could never master it. Any faggot made by me would be loose and likely to fall apart.) Friday would be baking day, more wood in smaller lengths this time, put into a huge baker's oven.

The Union at Tenterden.

The oven had to be got white hot by stoking it with wood, then the ashes were scraped out and the baking began. The whole week's baking was done at one time, bread, cakes, pies, the lot. All was done the same day. How they kept things fresh in the summer I do not know, but they seemed to have all sorts of wrinkles which we do not need to use today with our modern gadgets. I do remember Auntie Bea saying they used to put food in a watertight tin and put it in the well. Those baker's ovens were really economical. Once hot, they stayed hot and food could be placed in different parts for different temperatures.

The copper was really copper, and after use was cleaned and polished until one could see one's face in it. I have had one of these coppers and beautiful they look when polished. Nowadays, they are bought by dealers and are quite valuable. I had one where I was in service. It was kept for logs for the fire.

My great grandparents were tenant farmers renting a small farm from a big estate at Shadoxhurst, near Woodchurch. It seemed they had to be very careful how they behaved, and not do anything that could offend the estate owner.

During the time mother worked in the fields, she became friendly with a young man, a nephew of one of the landowners in the village. It had to be a secret, although her brothers were in the know. Like any such clandestine meeting it was bound to be found out. The first thing mother knew was when the landowner called to see her grandmother to demand that her granddaughter never spoke to his nephew again. As a tenant farmer she was in no position to refuse. In any case, she was shocked that it had been going on 'under her nose' as she said.

The next thing mother knew, the young man was sent off to Rhodesia, while mother was left to face the music and finally to have to admit to being pregnant. Mother always said the man would have married her as he had promised, but I am not so sure. I will never have anything but contempt for my father. I was one of the persons most hurt by being illegitimate. My great grandmother was furious. It brought disgrace on the whole house. She said that she hung her head in shame whenever she met anyone she knew. No doubt she did, but the fact remained

Hop pickers about 1870, by G.J. Pinwell. The scene changed little over the next fifty years. (Maidstone Museum)

that she herself had sent her own daughter to live with a man, to tend his brood, knowing full well that the man had three children and only two bedrooms.

I think that a lot of this righteous indignation was sheer hypocrisy and a cloak to hide her own guilt in the whole sorry business. When mother became more noticeable, she was sent out and told not to come back again. This sounds dreadful today, when most mothers would stand by their girl in such an event. In those days this often happened. Indeed, I can remember a girl I went to school with being turned out one night and having to go to the Union at ten o'clock at night. The parents did relent afterwards and have her back again. The baby disappeared. It was said that she had gone to a relative who was childless.

Mother had to walk the long way from Shadoxhurst to the Union at Tenterden. I can imagine the turmoil she felt as she walked along, cast off by everyone, scorned by those who could have shown sympathy. Mother said that she felt like looking for the nearest pond and ending it all. The nearer she got the worse she felt. She was terrified at what was going to happen to her. I myself wake up sometimes with a feeling that something terrible is going to happen. It never does, and I now take it in my stride, but I am sure it is a legacy of that walk poor mother had to Tenterden that day.

In the workhouse, mother kept working until I was born and afterwards was allowed to see me for feed times. Otherwise, I was in the nursery with Fan. As I became older, mother was allowed to see me once a week only, but I don't remember that. When the summer came great grandmother needed mother to help on the farm as one of the brothers had gone away to work as a groom.

Mother was allowed out to do this if she took me with her. Of course I do not remember anything of this, only what I have gathered from talking to my mother.

As soon as the harvest was in, once again mother was sent back to the workhouse. The next year it was the same, and the next, but at the end of that season mother was found a place at Wye College in service. I was kept by my great grandmother this time. Mother was doing well there and had saved up quite a bit of money which she gave to her grandmother for my keep. Poor woman, she couldn't win. She was nothing more than a slave as all money was taken away from her. There at college she became friendly with a student. She should have learned her lesson from the last time, but I suppose a little kindness made her forget that the other man had left her in the lurch. The fact remains that she was again pregnant and the student was missing.

It was the same sorry story all over again and she remained in the Union until she was sixty-eight when I was allowed to have her to live with me. I had tried to have her with me as soon as I had sufficient room for her, but it was never allowed by the Board of Guardians. When she did come, it was too late. She was institutionalised by then and in all the seventeen years I had her she was never really at ease with me and treated me as a sort of authority over her.

Chapter 3

EARLY DAYS AT SMALLHYTHE

Auntie Bea was deeply religious and every Sunday, wet or fine, snow or hail, off we would go to church in the little hamlet of Smallhythe. I had never been to a church service before. The singing was all right, but oh those long, long prayers, kneeling on a hard hassock with a poke in my back every time I fidgeted, which was pretty often. I soon began to find something to occupy my mind while the prayers were in progress.

At Christmas time, the pews were all woven with holly, ivy and other seasonal decorations. During the prayers, I whiled away the time with sticking holly berries on to the jet ornament on Auntie's hat. Her devotions must have been very sincere because she never felt me doing this, and after church she couldn't understand it when people remarked on her original hat trim. Going home, Uncle said he hadn't seen that hat before. Auntie became even more perplexed and couldn't think what everyone was on about. I was getting a bit worried by now and was quite expecting a good scolding when she found out. However, as soon as I got in I was made to go and change my socks as I had walked in a puddle on the way home. Auntie Bea threw her hat on the bed and went to get me a clean pair of socks so I took the opportunity to take all those berries off and throw them out of the window. She never found out and could never understand the mystery, so I got out of that scrape all right.

King George's coronation took place two years after I went to live with the couple. It was a great occasion for the village. Everyone was asked to dress their children in white, if possible, and they were to be taken by horse and wagon to Tenterden to the recreation field for a big tea party. Auntie went to a great deal of trouble to get me a dress. Money was tight. There was an allowance for clothes for me once a quarter, but I was growing very fast. It was as much as they could do to keep up with new boots. There wasn't much left over for new clothes. However, Auntie did her best and made me a white cotton dress trimmed with Broderie Anglaise. It was a lovely dress, at least in my eyes. It had three large insets of the lace, one on the yoke, one on the waist and a huge flounce of it at the hem. This was threaded through with red, white and blue ribbons. In all my life I had never had anything like it. There was a little hat to match, threaded with the same ribbon. I could hardly wait for the great day and was forever peeping in the cupboard to look at it.

The day before the great day, Auntie Bea went to the farmer across the field to get a pair of white boots which his child had outgrown. While she was away I again peeped at my lovely dress, and alas for me I just had to try it on, and then I just had to feel what it was like to walk out in it. I only went a little way out in the field at the back of the house, when I saw Auntie leaving the farm door.

Smallhythe Church. The cottage on the left later burned down.

I hurried back indoors, but alas my hurry was my undoing. I slipped on the grass, and horror of horrors, there was a big green stain on the back of the dress. Now if only I had owned up to what I had done there might have been time to do something about it. Instead, I hid it back in the cupboard. The next day I was bathed, my straight hair put in curlers and sat on a chair and was told to sit still till they were both ready. At last the moment came and I was by now terribly frightened. Suppose I couldn't go to the tea party? Auntie Bea looked at the dress in horror. Any punishment I needed I got at that moment as she looked first at the dress and then at me. Nothing could be done about it at this late time. I would have to wear my best dress; this was dark blue, quite nice really, but nothing like as good as the new one. 'I don't know whether they will allow you in with a dark dress' she said, so off we went with many misgivings. Every child had been asked to attend the party in a white dress. One lady said 'couldn't you manage a white dress' and Auntie said there had been a mishap to it. Everyone said 'what a pity'. No one knew it was me. I dare say they thought Auntie Bea couldn't manage to make one. They all knew I was a Union child. That was what was so nice about my dear old couple, they stood by me in everything.

At the teaparty, I sat on a stool and was plied with food until I could eat no more. I remember eating a lovely tart with such a nice looking middle. I nibbled the pastry all round savouring the thought of that delicious centre at last. 'Take that away from that little girl; she doesn't like it' someone said, and I lost my lovely tart. I was handed the plate again, so I went to take the same sort. 'Oh no' said the man, 'you don't like those', so I had to choose another sort. I never got my special cake. When I told Auntie afterwards, she said it was a punishment for being such a naughty girl.

I began to feel very frightened about God at this time. The fact that he was up there watching all I did was very alarming. The only fault I could find with

'Every child had been asked to attend the party in a white dress.'

Auntie Bea was her strict attitude to religion. I wonder how many children are brought up in fear of the everlasting fires of hell? I was terrified of God. To me he was an ogre, who reigned above us, saw all we did and would send me to hell. I had done enough to be sent there already. Dear old Uncle said one day that she was frightening me. You can't put old heads on young shoulders, he said. Perhaps he had a talk with her later because Auntie Bea began to talk about God being a God of love. Eventually I got a more rational idea of God, so things were easier. The sabbath was still the day for devotions and little else, unless it was to visit the sick or my mother. I did fear God as someone to mete out punishment and I was often afraid to do things as he would be watching me. On Sundays no toy was to be touched, nothing sung except hymns, not even a flower was allowed to be picked.

One day we were going to visit my mother which we did every alternate Sunday. Outside visiting was allowed on Sundays and Wednesdays. I hung behind to pick some primroses to take to my mother. When Auntie Bea saw what I was doing, she promptly made me throw them all away. I was very upset and kept looking back at them with their petals ruffling in the breeze. I did not understand it then and neither do I now, but that was Auntie's belief and it had to be obeyed. When we returned, they were still lying on the ground, but I was not allowed to pick them up, even though I said they were going to die.

Auntie said I should have thought of that before, so it was my own fault. I felt even worse then, and felt very guilty about them. I have always had a very

Dame Ellen Terry.
(photo by courtesy of the National Trust)

strong conscience which is a bit of a nuisance at times, but no doubt it has kept me on the straight and narrow, so I should really be thankful for it.

Near to the church at Smallhythe was a beautiful house owned by the then great Shakespearian actress Ellen Terry, later to become Dame Ellen Terry. Often she would come down to the cottage to stay for a while and would use the time to be photographed with various people of the village. Auntie Bea used to look after the little girl of the caretaker during the time that the actress was in residence, so I often talked with the great lady. Once she sat me on her lap and said what a funny little thing I was, so it seemed I was still no better in looks. I suppose she had a press agent with her as she was always having photographs taken and once or twice it was with me.

The cottage we lived in was in the heart of the country. I had to go across two fields to get to the lane and then there was a long walk to reach the main road. My way to school led me past a wood and running up through this wood was a set of stones leading to a meadow at the top. These steps were called Jacob's Ladder, and no matter how late I was going to school, I always went up those steps. I have been back to see them many times since, but they don't seem anything like as steep as they used to.

I never really fitted in with the children at Smallhythe school. I had spent four years of life going from pillar to post and it took a long, long time for me to adjust: in fact it has taken the best part of my life. Auntie had quite a time placating angry mothers who complained I had kicked their child. I did this because all the children in the workhouse kicked out at anyone who upset them. It was the only kind of protest they knew. There was plenty for me to kick out

Ellen Terry's cottage at Smallhythe.

about. I was a misfit and it would have taken people much more skilled in the knowledge of the human mind to help me unravel than my dear old couple. Nevertheless, they came to love me and I them, so with them the barrier was overcome.

At Christmas time our teacher used to tell us all to hide our eyes and when we looked there on the shelf was a row of toys, one for each of the good pupils. There was one for everyone except me, and I went home and cried most of the night. Auntie went to see the teacher, because although she knew I was not a well behaved child, Auntie felt that a little more help from the teacher might have helped. Instead, she was making it worse. This teacher really was trying to help me. She thought it might have made me realise that being good brought its reward. She was very upset when she found out how miserable it had made me.

A few days later, she came to see me to ask if I could help her with her own decorations as she had been too busy at school to do them before. My importance knew no bounds as I went to help her. I was the one chosen, and I had never before been chosen to do anything. I got on a lot better in the new term, although I still did very naughty things. I also got on better with the other children, so I think the teacher must have had a word with one of the parents who had said that I must not play with her little girl. I became friendly with one or two, and the friendships have lasted through school life and after. It was to take all my school years for me to become as normal as other children, although I did not realise it then. I was feeling insecure due mainly to the circumstances of my birth.

Chapter 4

A MOVE TO TENTERDEN

As he grew older Uncle still went to work, breaking up stones for the road repairs. A huge pile of large stones would be put by the road side and he would go with a big hammer and break them into a suitable size for the repairs. It was a very hard job, so he and Auntie Bea began to look for a cottage nearer the town where he might get a job in gardening. The cottages were easy to get then, so a place was found behind Tenterden High Street. I was sent to stay with Auntie Bea's parents while the move took place. Her parents had a small farm which they rented. I loved the farm. There were chickens to feed, and pigs and cows. The family were against Auntie Bea having me at all. They thought she was the wrong type of person to look after me, and perhaps they were right, but there was nothing they could do about it. They also disapproved of her marrying a man much older than she was, but again they could do nothing to stop it. I must admit that they were always very kind to me except the youngest sister. I was very much afraid of her, though I am sure it was a case of her bark being worse than her bite. I got to know her very well later on in life. Gran, as I called Auntie Bea's mother, was a sweet old lady. In the morning she would allow me to help skim the cream off the night's milk. This always fascinated me. The cream was taken off with a skimmer (a ladle with holes in it). The cream would crinkle up on top of the milk. Usually Aunt Kit would come in and I would be sent out, down on the farm, where there was a huge bin filled with maize from which I fed the chickens. I loved it on that farm. Later on they moved to an old house on the other side of the road. This was a very old place and was reputed to have been built by a Dutch man who had been shipwrecked at Smallhythe when the sea came up as far as that. I can remember a Dutch man living there who was called Mr Van Lan Shouton, or a name similar. He was supposed to be a descendant of the original man. The house was called Dutch Cottage and some of the beams do look as if they could have been made from ship beams. It still stands to this day. Auntie Bea's parents bought the place when the Dutch man went back to his forefathers' home. I have stayed in this place and very interesting it is with some of the beams cut to look like portholes.

Our new home was a nice cottage. I loved living near the shops and seeing people every time I went out, but I missed the old cottage. I soon became aware that people were not as kind to me as at the old place. Children living in the town were far more forward and self reliant than I was, having been shut off as it were from civilisation except for school and the farmer's wife across the field.

My new school took a lot of getting used to. Auntie Bea was old fashioned and so was I in my way of talking. The other children were always making fun of me. The old naughty ways came back again and I was always in trouble. I just

Dutch Cottage at Morgnew, near Smallhythe.

couldn't help being naughty. I believe it was because I was confused and unhappy. Anyone who has the care of children of a broken marriage will probably know what I mean. Once again I had to get used to a different sort of outlook. Also, I realised Auntie Bea was not as other girls' mothers. I was not old enough to analyse it then, but I did know something somewhere was different.

I got into all sorts of scrapes. On one occasion, the master of the school had me in front of the whole school and gave me the cane. He said afterwards that I was the first girl he had caned, and I am sure it was so. He really seemed upset.

Eventually, I did settle down but not before many heartbreaks, both mine and theirs who taught me. Perhaps then would have been the time for me to have been removed from the care of the old couple, before I became more and more moulded into their ways. In spite of all that, they were, until their death, my truest friends. Everyone has a right to behave as they wish provided they don't break any law and they would never do that. They gave me the thing I needed most, love, just at a time when I was feeling insecure.

Uncle still went to work, but in a nearby garden. Auntie Bea used to do seasonal work in the fields, with the people she had worked with at Smallhythe. During the summer holidays I went with her and I well remember a special day when all the women were grumbling because a farmer nearby had given his workers a small rise. They were to have 6/- a week for a 5½ day week. Where Auntie Bea worked, it was 5/- for a 5½ day week's work. As Auntie was the only one not in a tied cottage, she was asked to approach the farmer about a rise. He used to come round every day, riding on a big white horse. This day, she asked if she might speak to him, and while the others worked as if they had nothing to do with what she was saying, Auntie Bea asked for more money. 'We can't afford

A typical farm horse.

to give our men meat' she said, 'only once a week and that is a little beef for a pie. Our men go to work on suet pudding and Oxo' she said. 'Nonsense' said the farmer, 'suet pudding is good enough for any working man. They don't want meat.' He then rode on.

The women were very upset, but no one dared to say anything to the farmer as they lived under him, and they could be put out of their cottages if the farmer so wished. It did have a happy ending however, for on the Saturday, the women got a 6d rise and Auntie Bea got notice that she was not needed again. When Uncle heard the story he said 'Old woman, never vote Conservative. They only look after themselves and get rich at our expense'. Soon after this Uncle gave up work. He was now very old and they lived for a time on Auntie Bea's savings. One day he said that he would like me to have a rolling pin which he had cut out of a holly tree on the day he married his first wife. It was dark brown with age, but seemed to roll out better than anything one could buy in a shop. 'It will last out you, your children and their children' he said. Later in life, when I married, I was given the rolling pin which I have used every day until the day my eldest got married, when I passed it on to her. She in turn has passed it on to her daughter on her wedding day, and it is still in use. By now it has become an heirloom.

Uncle had a daughter and a son by his first marriage. The son had married and had two children. The daughter still lived at Smallhythe, at the Ferry Cottage.

Smallhythe in 1905. The handwriting is Ellen Terry's.
(photo by courtesy of the National Trust)

Her husband had to open the gate to anyone wanting to go through the toll gate. At one time the sea had come up to his place and the toll gate still remained for some time after I left Smallhythe. There was a card in the porch which told the scale of charges, so much for a wagon, so much for a trap, and so on. There was also a little path which pedestrians walked without paying.

At the time I was ten years old, Uncle's son died and his wife abandoned her children and left the house with the husband lying dead and the two children, one of five and one of ten. A neighbour got in touch with Uncle and the little girls were brought home to us. This was a very awkward situation for us all as the cottages only had two bedrooms and the rule was that all foster children had to have a room to themselves. Arrangements were made for the oldest to go to her aunt who wanted to adopt her. In the case of the youngest it was a different matter. An old friend of Auntie's family wished to adopt the small one, but this took time as it had to be done legally with the mother giving her consent. Meanwhile, we were overcrowded and that was against the rules, so I had to leave. A few days later I was told that I was to have a new home. It was a tearful parting. I had just begun to settle down. School was a lot easier and I was fitting in with the other children. Now, I had to go through yet another change and the two whom I had grown to love were to be left behind. The irony was that just two weeks later, the little girl went to the people who were to adopt her and Auntie was without anyone again.

Chapter 5

NEW FOSTER PARENTS, AND AN INTRODUCTION TO HOP-PICKING

My new home was a sweet shop in High Street, Tenterden. It was a ghastly mistake. Everyone said I would be happy, but they couldn't have been more wrong. The new foster parents had just lost a little boy and friends suggested taking in another child to help them get over it. Perhaps if I had been a pretty little thing it might have worked out, or if I had been with more rational outlooking people previously, then I might have settled in with them.

In no way could I come up to the standard of the little son. In all fairness, I must admit they did their best for me. The first thing they did was to buy me new clothes. That must have cost something, as the allowance they received was very small and had been spent in rigging me out ready for the move. However, most of the clothes were considered unsuitable. Auntie Bea always bought things two sizes too big, to allow for growing, she said. Also she always went in for very dark, serviceable clothes. I was very pleased with my new outfits, but I soon found out that there was a snag in wearing nice clothes. I was one of those people who need only look at mud and it promptly comes up and sticks on me. It still does even now. I can be walking with a friend, both of us doing our best to avoid the mud patches – my friend will emerge clean and I will be splashed with mud.

I soon came to realise that there was a difference between the family's own little girl and me when she went to kiss her dad goodnight. I went to do the same but found it was discouraged. Apart from that, I was treated the same, fed the same, given a sweet at the same time. I also went for a walk with them on a Sunday, after first taking flowers down to the little boy's grave. I had my first glimpse of the sea while I was with them. We went to Hastings by coach – char-à-banc it was called in those days. As we went down the hill to the sea front, I could see some ships, and to me it looked as if they were in the air.

I did enjoy my paddle, but of course being me, I had to get my best dress wet. In every way they tried to make something of me, but it was no good. I could not fit in and that, coupled with the fact that I could never hope to take the place of their little boy, made it bad for both of us.

About this time I became aware of the stigma attached to the nature of my birth. I had settled down more or less at school. I changed from the British school which I had been attending and went to the National one. Here I had new friends. I seemed to get on better with them. I was not allowed to bring anyone home, as the daughter did, but I did go out to play with my friends after I had done my little jobs on the Saturday morning. I had to clean the knives, a job I hated. Some of the knives were very worn at the tips and seemed to bend over a bit. I had to rub two bits of Bathbrick together to make a powder and spread it

The sweetshop at Tenterden today.

on the knife board, then rub and rub until they were quite clean. I also had to do the cellar steps down as well and clean my room. Then I was free to go out to play, so it was up to me to do it as quickly and as well as I could, but it always had to be inspected first, and that was where the trouble began. I never could do it properly the first time. I always had to do it over until I did do it right. I really did store up trouble for myself.

We had a new girl come to school and I soon became friendly with her. Now although I used to play with other girls outside, no one asked me to their home, but this new girl did. Her mother was very nice to me and I had a lovely time playing with my new friend's toys. The next day I called for her on my way to school, but was told she was not ready, and I was not to wait for her. Then when I did see her, she said that she was not to play with me anymore as I was born in disgrace. I could not understand it, but when I told my foster parents, they said they could, as it was true. I had been born in disgrace and I could not expect respectable people to treat me as themselves.

The same thing happened at school. If the nicest girls spoke to me they would always make sure never to be seen doing so if they were near their own home. I had plenty of friends though to play with, but the stigma remained for many years.

At school, the master asked once what we intended to do when we left school. He went right along the row asking each one as he came to them. When he got to

The pump where Dorothy and other hop-pickers were collected by wagon to be taken to Pick Hill Farm.

me he said 'You haven't got a choice. All workhouse children will be put in domestic service.' I suppose he was right, but he might have let me say what I would like to be. Everybody seemed bent on rubbing it in that I was not like others and had no say in my future at all.

In the Autumn, I was booked half a bin with a farmer for the hop picking. We were picked up by a wagon at the Old Pump at the East end of the High Street, and taken to the farm at Pickhill. Here the owner read out the rules. They had to be very religiously adhered to, and a fine of one penny was taken for every breach. Anyone not cleaning their hops ready for the measurer when he came to take out the hops could be paid off at once. I cannot understand how it was I wasn't. I always kept him waiting while I had a frantic clean out of the bin. Perhaps the man liked the chance of a pause to smoke his pipe, for he always let me off with dire threats as to what would happen next time. All the money was to be spent on my clothes so I should have tried harder, but at ten years old, it's a lot nicer to go off to play. I did not dare do that, or I would have been stood off, but the children who did not have a bin and whose mothers were not so strict would come and play with me. The pole puller did his best by telling them to go away, as I had work to do, but he couldn't be there all the time and back would come the children again. I started off in the morning with determination to pick hard all day, but I was always tempted and would play about unless the pole puller saw me, then I would work well for a while. He was a nice man, that pole puller; he gave me many an apron full of hops. The men always wore a hessian

Transporting the hops.

apron with a huge pocket. This was to put all the hops that were dropped when he pulled up the poles. Hops were all tied in those days, and each was trained up a pole, set in three to a hill. At least they were on that farm. Some farmers had them closer and one pole to a hill. Then, women went along in May and twisted three bines to a pole, tying them to the pole with a dried rush. Nowadays hops are all grown up a string. (I did a lot of hop tying and training later on when I was married. In fact, it was the source from which I paid my winter doctor's bills for myself and children. There was no free medical attention except for the working person.) The rushes they would get earlier so that they were sere and pliable. I did earn enough to buy my new coat, but only because my foster parents came on a Wednesday afternoon to help me. I think they enjoyed the change. I worked better when they were there as the other girls did not come along to hinder me.

On Saturday and on the last day, we either got a catch or gave a large bushel. The bin is always left empty over the weekend, so if there was half a bushel left at the end of the measuring, then it would be taken and called a bushel. This was a catch, and we youngsters always hoped ours would be a catch and that we would not have to give an extra big bushel instead. I believe that measurer felt sorry for me, for I always got a catch.

At the end of a year, my foster parents decided fostering me had been a mistake, and asked the lady who acted as the Union's agent to find me another home. This agent's job was to pay the money for the keep each week, to see that the child was being looked after properly, and to pay out the money for clothing once a quarter. Also once a quarter the local doctor came. He always rode in a carriage driven by a coachman. He never knocked on the door, but would open it and shout 'send that girl out to me, hurry.' I later had occasion to be very grateful to him and see another side of his character.

I know my foster parents did their very best for me, but it wasn't any good. I couldn't settle and I was very unhappy. On Fridays at school, we always sang a special hymn: 'God that madest earth and heaven, darkness and light'. I used to feel so sad as I sang that and can still feel the same if I hear it sung today. So I left then. They must have been as pleased to see me go as I was to go.

I needed a lot of corners knocked off me, and it took a long time. When I think about it now, I must have been a very bewildered little girl, and the only way I could retaliate was to do something outrageous. This in turn would bring down the wrath of foster parents and teachers alike.

It really stemmed from the fact that I was different. Everyone said so. I seemed to have no rights, no privileges as others did. I had been, in my short life, back and forth, from Union to great gran's farm, to Auntie Bea at four, to my second foster parents and now at ten was to move again. An unsettled early life, the stigma of being illegitimate and not realising why I was despised because of it, all combined to make me grow up with the feeling that everyone was against me. I had a huge inferiority complex and it has taken the best part of my life to conquer. In fact I still have it but I can control it now.

Chapter 6

THE FIRST WORLD WAR BECOMES A REALITY

My new foster parents were quite different from the last ones. They had one son who was in the army. The war had started while I was with Auntie Bea. I was coming home from school one day when a woman went by crying that we were at war. 'We shall all be overrun by the Germans' she said. I ran home expecting to see a German lurking around the corner. It's surprising how soon we got used to seeing soldiers, and in no time we were carrying on normally. Except for the soldiers, we were the same as before. It was sometime later that we found out what war was.

Aunt Kit, my new foster parent, was very kind to me. I was allowed a lot of freedom. I lived as they did and was given a nice room to myself. On the wall was a lovely picture of a girl with long brown hair and a huge basket of daffodils. I loved that picture. The house, Yew Tree Cottage in Tenterden High Street, was quite big. It had four rooms on the ground floor, four bedrooms on the next with three attic rooms at the top. Soon after I got there a telegram boy came to the door. As soon as Aunt Kit saw it she began to cry. I went to get the telegram but she couldn't open it as she was sure what was in it, so I had to as she feared it was to say her only boy was dead. It was a dreadful moment. Uncle was doing the rounds as he was a postman, and Aunt was sitting in the chair moaning. I got a neighbour in because I did not know what to do. The telegram was not from the War Office but from a woman who said she was his wife. This turned out to be true, but was the first either of them knew about his marriage. When Uncle came in he took over, and sent a telegram to the wife inviting her to come and stay with them. This she did, bringing with her a baby of a few weeks old.

The shock to those two must have been terrific, but they made her welcome. It wasn't long before she was going around with the soldiers. It was evident that she was not a nice woman. Finally, they got her a cottage in another part of the town as there was always friction between the two women. I expect Aunt thought that all the secrecy was the wife's fault and the wife thought Aunt was making a fuss out of nothing. It was natural really to think only good of her boy, especially as he was dead.

The baby was sweet. I often used to go down to look after it while she went out to see some soldier or other. Finally she had them in the house and I was stopped from going down there.

Until now, we had not seen anything of the actual war. Then, one afternoon, we were coming home from school when we heard a droning noise overhead. Some women ran by shouting 'Run home, get under cover'. The next minute there was a very big bang. We didn't need more telling, we rushed home as fast

Tenterden High Street early this century.

as we could. We could hear the planes as we ran. They were not overhead, but they sounded alarming enough to us. There were more bangs as we went in the door. My friend came with me. Poor girl, she was terrified. She had been evacuated to us from Belgium. We had two families of them but the other ones were older. My friend was very badly shell-shocked. Any little excitement and she would start stamping her foot. She couldn't help it and it wasn't anger, only excitement. We had to get her mother in to her as she was petrified with fear. I began to realise what war was and the results of it. A little later it was brought home to me in a way I will never forget.

Aunt woke me during the night. 'Come and see' she said, 'there is a German Zeppelin coming down.' I went outside and there in the sky, quite close, was a big airship all in flames. As I watched it burst into fire all over and I could see the undercarriage where the men were sitting. They must have been burning alive as I watched. The greatest horror to me was that all around me I could hear people cheering and as it suddenly lurched and fell to the ground out of sight, the biggest cheer I had ever heard went up. I couldn't stay out any longer. To me it was all too dreadful. All around people were enthusing about the Zeppelin being brought down. All I could think of was those men being burned alive while we stood and watched and cheered. I know it wasn't the men they were thinking about, but the destroying of an enemy ship, but I could never reconcile myself to be cheerful at anyone's downfall. It could be happening to our men in their country, but two wrongs don't make a right. It seemed to me it makes really nice people into savages.

The Tannery, Smallhythe Road, which could be smelled all over the town.
(photo by courtesy of Tenterden Museum)

There were two or three other incidents which brought home to me the other side of war. We had a very nice man living in our town, a retired army officer, who was also one of our school governors. Whenever we saw him he would be whistling, always cheerful, always with a cheery word for everyone. He would help anyone in need, so it was with great surprise that I heard he had shot himself, following a bout of the dreadful epidemic of flu raging over the whole country at that time.

It later turned out that with Germany likely to win the war, all his money was lost. Every child at school contributed to a wreath and I, with three others, was delighted to take it to his lodgings on the morning of the funeral. There were a lot of wreaths with red, white and blue ribbons on, because of his army service. A few days later a policeman called at the school to find out who had been stealing the ribbons, which had all disappeared from the grave. 'Stand up all those who have been near the cemetery over the weekend' said the policeman. At least half the school stood up. The cemetery was a favourite place for getting together to look and see who had the best graves. We also used to water graves for people who found it too far to walk. We need not have worried however, as the culprits were soon discovered, actually wearing the ribbons. They were a very poor family, looked down on by many, just as I had been looked down upon by those who thought it such a disgrace to be a child of an unmarried mother. We didn't hear anything about it and the ribbons disappeared from the children's hair.

Another aspect of the war was the blackout. I loved it, it was great fun to be out in it. We could be excused for bumping into people, which we often did intentionally. We always said we were sorry but the fact remained that we did do it on purpose. What joy we found in it. I can't understand why, but it was one of our favourite pastimes at that time.

Another very dreadful thing happened as a direct result of the war. Opposite us lived a very pleasant woman. She had three nicely-spoken children as well. Her husband was by now a prisoner of war and had been for about a year. She became very friendly with the widow of Aunt's son who now lived round the corner from the woman. Before long the wounded soldiers were going daily into the nice woman's house. One day on coming home from school, there were quite a lot of people outside her house, all talking in whispers. They stopped when we approached, but we were soon to hear the dreadful news. The poor woman had become pregnant by one of the wounded soldiers, and she had taken something to get rid of the baby. Instead, she herself became very ill and after two days of anxious waiting the poor woman died. The children were sent to a relative and the home was broken up. We did hear that there was going to be trouble for the person who gave her the poison, but we never heard any more. It was just another incident, the result of war.

There was another aspect of the war, although of a happier nature. At school a man came to talk to us about it and in what way we could help. He told us about the ships and how they had to run the gauntlet of the enemy ships to bring us our food. He told us that if we were to eat one slice of bread a meal less, we would help the war effort, by sending less ships to get our food. He had a form with him for us to sign. On it was stated that all who had signed would eat at least one slice a day less. Of course I was one who said I would sign and when I got home, Aunt said 'all right, you will have one piece less' and I did right to the end. I now had one whole slice right across the loaf and one half slice – that was for tea. At breakfast, I had bread and milk which I had to collect from a farm a good mile away, before I could go to school. It was skim milk but was very good. It was skimmed by hand and cost 1d against 2½d for the new milk. Dinner was a Foster Clark's soup square, with potatoes and a rice pudding made from skim milk.

On Saturday and Sunday we all had the same food, always a roast on Sunday. We really didn't do so badly for war time.

I could have done with that extra slice of bread at tea-time though – I wouldn't be in such a hurry to fill in forms again.

Chapter 7

MISCHIEF

I had settled down a lot better now. Very few people made comments about my birth, so I gradually felt more at home with others. I did get into a lot of scrapes though, especially in church. One of the things I have never liked was the long drawn out prayers which seem to be the usual thing in a church service. We children soon found something to while away the time during the prayers. We were expected to go to the morning service up until the hymn after the prayers, and before the sermon started we were conducted out by our Sunday school teacher under cover of the singing of the hymn.

One particular day, I had spent the prayer time tying my boot laces to those of the girl next to me. She in turn tied hers to the ones next to her and so on all down the row. Now, whether the prayers were shorter that day or we were so engrossed in what we were doing, I do not know, but suddenly it was time to go out and there we were all tied together. The Sunday school teacher, a dear elderly lady, whom we all loved, tried to get us out quietly, but the more she tried, the more we became agitated – there never was such a row in that church before. Some of us were vainly trying to undo our laces while others were trying to get out. The lady in the row behind us was poking me in the back, and our poor little teacher was by now getting more and more frantic as the time went by. The verger came to see what was wrong. Suddenly the vicar realised what it was and in a loud voice said 'sit down'. We then all had to get back in again which was nearly as bad as trying to get out, but in the end we were all in the pews again and sat still as mice.

After the sermon, on his way back to the altar, he said 'stay there'. This we did with some alarm. No one had meant to stay tied up till the end of prayers. It was just that we were caught off our guard. The service was over and the vicar came over and demanded to know who the ringleader was. Well, I had tied the first lace, so I had to take the blame, but I didn't expect the others to have followed suit. I had to go and see the vicar the next day. He was really a very nice gentleman, and we were all very fond of him. He talked quite a bit about behaving properly in God's house, and gave a little homily about trying to understand the prayers. He was really very good considering how I and my friends had upset the church routine. He shook hands and said he was sure I would not play that trick again. I was going out feeling very determined never to misbehave again when the vicar's daughter came out. She was quite different and told me I was a disgrace to the whole Sunday school. If she had but known it she undid all that her father had done. We never got on, she and I. To her mind, I was an undisciplined, unruly girl. I know she thought I would end up a wrong 'un, she often said so. Those who were always well behaved got on well with her, but she never had any time for those who did not conform to her pattern, and I did not. I am afraid she always brought out the worst in me while her dear old father brought out the best.

I had another brush with the vicar's daughter. We were all expected to put money in the collection. In my case, it was paid for my Uncle. He gave me 6d a week. This was 2d for bank, 2d for spending and 1d each for church collections and Sunday school. Now on the way to Sunday school we used to go to the back door of a sweet shop and spend ½d of the money. I had no excuse, I knew it was not my money to spend, but I would go along with the others and spend my ½d as well. The shop owner knew what money we were spending too, but she was quite willing to take it. One Sunday morning the shop keeper said she couldn't sell to us. We had no idea why until the next day when the vicar said 'Would all the children who have been in the habit of visiting the shop on the way to church please come to the vicarage after school.' We now knew why we had not been served in the shop. Six of us went along, but there were at least ten who used to spend their offertory money there. This time the vicar was very stern. He talked about the danger of petty stealing and of how much could be done with the ½d we had used over quite a long time. We had robbed the poor and the missionaries who were trying to teach the heathen to learn about God. I think we were all ashamed of ourselves. I know I was. He asked what we thought we could do to put matters right. I offered to give my 2d a week pocket money, but the vicar said no, it must be something more than money. He arranged to give us a job which would take all our pleasure time for quite a while. We were to help him in his garden until all of a new bit of ground had been dug. It was hard work and my hands were blistered, but we were paid so much for each hour we worked and this we handed over to the vicar who signed for it. The piece of ground was to be planted with vegetables which we would grow and the money was to be sent to the missionary fund. We got really interested in that garden, and even after our stint was over we did not like anyone else to do any of it. Once the ground was dug our penance was over, and it was cultivated by the school as a whole, as one of our school projects.

I was still not able to shine in anything at school. I could not do a nice needlework piece. My garments always had to be sold off cheaply. I would stroke the gathers until I made little ladders in the material. I couldn't paint, nor knit. My socks had ladders in too, not from stroking but from dropped stitches. Then the vicar's daughter said she needed so many girls and boys to help in a big missionary exhibition she was putting on. All the good needleworkers were soon busy making things and the boys were doing fretwork. I wasn't good at anything. I told my Sunday school teacher about it, and she said she was sure that if I genuinely wanted to do something, then I only had to pray and she was sure God would find something for me to do. Well I tried hard enough that night, and the next day went along expecting to hear of something I could do. The vicar's daughter came in to see how we were all getting on with what was being done. Then she turned to me and said 'if you had applied your mind to doing things useful such as needlework, you would have been able to have the satisfaction of

Acting in a school pantomime. Dorothy is on the right, wearing a dark dress.

having done a good job for the missionary works, the same as the others.' She went on to say I would grow up a useless girl. I thought she was very unkind and I still do. If she had tried to find out why I did naughty things, and why I was not good at things she thought were most important, then we might have got on better. As it was she still continued to rub me up the wrong way and always did, even when I was grown up. However, I did get a chance to do something for the missionary exhibition. They were also putting on a play in the evening of that day and needed another one to be a Chinese girl. Most of the people acting in this were friends of the vicar or his daughter. No-one from the school was taking part. Two days before the event, one of those who was taking the part of a Chinese was taken ill and the schoolmaster was asked to find her a substitute at short notice. They needed one who would look the part and one who could learn quickly, and that was me. I could learn very quickly. In the afternoon the vicar's daughter came and I went through the whole part without a mistake. I don't think she was very pleased, but perhaps it was me. I didn't think she would be. Anyhow, God answered my prayer. I really enjoyed acting; at last I was good at something. I have always liked acting in plays since.

My hair was brushed until it shone, and with a rhododendron in my hair and the real Chinese clothes, I really felt the part. I was the only child in that play and it did a lot for my ego. There was another play as well and some of the children were in that one.

Next door to us was a grocer's shop.' Yew Tree Cottage is on the left.

The great day came and went. There was a bit in the local paper about it and that really made it for us children. Not long after a missionary came to talk to us. He came quite regularly to tell us about the missionaries and what they did. Sometimes we had lantern slides. This was always a great treat for us but it would seem very tame today with all the cine-cameras, cinemas etc. There was a cinema in the town. I went once or twice, but money wasn't so free for things of that nature and of course it was always silent and black and white. We did find a few odd ways of making a little extra pocket money. One was at a May fair. This was one of the highlights of the year, always a school holiday. Most of us would have played truant anyhow, so they thought it best to make it a holiday instead.

We were up very early on the morning of the fair and off to meet the first farmer to help him drive his sheep. There weren't any big lorries to bring them in but just the farmers, the farmhands and anyone else who would lend a hand. We usually got 6d for gatting behind, and with loud shouts would herd the sheep into the field and into the pens. Then off again to find another farmer in need of help. Sometimes we would come unstuck and the farmer would say 'thank you' and that was all, but by and large we did pretty well out of it and got a meal as well. There was also a funfair where we spent our money. This was extra money which we could squander as we liked, and we did. Another thing special to the May fair was the lollypops. These were made by the woman owner of one of the sweet shops. They were lovely. No manufacturer could make them as she could. There were three kinds, peppermint with three stripes, clove with two and lemon with two red and one yellow stripe. These were still made long after the May fair had become a thing of the past, except that they came out at Easter instead. They were put on to birch twigs, 3 lollies to a branch, but could be sold separately.

I did have another source of income. Uncle always paid me ½d for each lot of manure I shovelled up from outside. Next door to us was a grocer's shop, and the grocer did his delivery by pony and trap. For quite a long time the pony would be tethered outside our house, so I could run out to pick up the manure. That continued until a boy came to live a few doors down. I didn't dare let him see me doing it.

Because of the war everyone by now either had people who usually lived in London, and could afford to take rooms in the safer places in the country, or if they did not, then those who had room billeted soldiers. We had two, very nice ones they were. One used to play the piano and we would get round it and sing. This was one of the nicest things of the war. Aunt also let two rooms to a lady and her grown up daughter. Soon after they came, the mother became very ill and died. It was very sad. They were the only living ones left out of a very large family. I went to her house, a long train journey away, to help her daughter sell up. It appears there was very little money left, so she would now be going out to find work. This she did and left us soon after the funeral.

I was still getting up to mischief. One of the things we all did was to run by the greengrocer's shop and snatch something off his display which he kept outside. Well, of course, being me, I was the one he finally caught with the telltale pea pod in my hand. He took me by the arm and said 'come along with me, we will go and see the policeman' and off I had to go, the pea pod still in my hand. All the way he talked about how small things led to bigger things, until by the time I was grown up, I would be a hardened criminal. I was shaking in my shoes. Then, just as he got to the police station, he said 'well goodbye little missie, remember what I have said.' He raised his hat and went away. The policeman was standing outside the station. 'What have you been up to, young varmint, run along or you will be late for school and don't do it again.' I didn't need telling twice. It's a lesson I never forgot.

Another bit of mischief we got up to was to go out in the blackout and tie the door handles of the houses together, then knock and run away. I had a lot of freedom as Aunt didn't seem to mind how much I went out or where I went or who I was with. One day the person responsible for looking after my welfare and reporting to the Board of Guardians how much I was progressing, said I was to be taught to do housework ready for service. I was now in my final year at school. I used to clean the brasses but not much else as by the time I had been to collect the milk from the farm and done the shopping there wasn't much time. Aunt preferred to do the housework, and I did the errands. It suited me and it suited her, but it did not train me for housework at all. I wasn't likely to get a job where I did the shopping.

When it was near my birthday, the person from the Board came and said I was to be sent to a home to be trained in domestic service. I was supplied with a tin trunk, a complete outfit of clothes and told to be ready on the morning of my birthday to catch the bus with her to go to a place at Maidstone. I went to take a tearful farewell of my dear old Aunt, still the one I loved the best, and early on the fateful morning, did my hair up in a bun. I had very fine hair so it was a little bun. It was quite common to leave school on the day one was fourteen. No-one expected to wait till end of term as happens now, and a girl put up her hair on the day she left school.

At 8 o'clock I set off with the agent to start another phase of my life. Never in all my fourteen years had I been consulted as to what I would like to do, nor told what I was to do until it was all settled.

Houses in Buckland Hill, Maidstone.

Chapter 8

THE MAIDSTONE TRAINING HOUSE

Thank goodness the outfit I had been given was not the same as the Board of Guardians gave to children who lived in the Union and came out to school each day, dressed in a sober frock and an awful round hat. I think it was the hat which I hated most. I had a tweed coat, one navy dress and one grey.

We arrived at about 11 o'clock on the doorstep of a house in Buckland Hill, Maidstone. The door was opened by a middle aged woman who looked at me and said 'so this is the new girl you have brought me.' No welcome, not even an 'I hope you are going to behave yourself'. I was quite used to that sort of greeting. Always wherever I went I was treated as a nobody. I should have been used to it by now but I still felt ill at ease as I followed the woman into the house.

There were eight girls in the home. One was a girl whose father was an officer in the army and in consequence was given preferential treatment. It appeared she had got herself into some sort of trouble and had been put there by her father as punishment. Her father had asked for her to be trained to work in a shop, but there wasn't any way she could get that sort of training there. It seemed she was lucky not to have been put into some sort of corrective detention, so I suppose it was the fact of who her father was which prevented that. I certainly learned more about the facts of life than I ever knew. That girl had certainly led a bad life. She wasn't a good companion for us, although she was very careful to say nothing in front of either of the people in charge. They thought she was more sinned against than sinned. We other girls could have told a different story, but none of us would. We loved to hear of the tales of the many boys she knew. As she was much older than we were, this girl was put in charge of us when we went out, as we were allowed to when we had finished our day's work. Every man and boy she met she chatted up. It was soon obvious to us why she so narrowly missed being sent away. The Matron of the home never found out, though, and a job was found for the girl in a dress shop in the town. Perhaps it was just as well for us that she did go or we might have become as bad as she was. We certainly lapped up all her tales. There were only two principals at the home, one the Matron and the other a much older woman who was supposed to have a bad heart. I cannot imagine she would have been in charge of a home if she was as bad as she said. We girls thought that it was just a way of trying to keep us behaving well when she was on duty. One day when we had been really rude to her and had dared to answer back when she had criticized what we were doing, she had gone to lie down because we had upset her so much. When a lady came to say that the church were putting on a special fete and were having a quick meeting to arrange it, and could she come along to it, up she got and off she went without any show of her former heart spasm.

The view over the allotments from Buckland Hill.

After giving strict instructions to the oldest girl to behave and keep us all behaving, she left. We loved to be on our own. It seemed to happen often. I cannot think that that home was at all the place to train girls. We had no real training, just did the daily routine. I had my own jobs, which were to do the drawing room and once a week to turn it out. This meant putting out every bit of furniture into the hall and then spreading tea leaves onto the carpet. This was supposed to bring up the colours. It might have done if the colour had not already been worn off it, but by then it was a dull dirt colour.

There was a chapel in the top of the house where we had to go before breakfast. It was a very high establishment. I had not been there long when the subject of Christening came up. Some of the girls were not baptised, so a mass Christening was arranged, followed by Confirmation. I had already been confirmed but as I had not got a baptism card to show I was christened again. We were all asked to go to confession. I had never heard of it before. I thought only Catholics went to confession, but no, we were sent to the chapel to meditate and then to write down all we had done wrong. As it was our first one, it meant all the sins I had or thought I had committed since I could remember. I could only think of the mischief which I had done as a child, but one of the girls, whom I had made my special friend, said we should put down all the things the girl had told us (the girl who had gone out to work in a shop and who had told us those tales which we were so ready to listen to). I expect she was right, because we knew we should not have listened to and sniggered at them, so I suppose it was a sin. We got together to decide how best to word it. Finally, we came up with having listened to disgusting stories. I can't think what the priest thought of us coming as we did from a very religious home. Apart from that I could only think of sweeping the dust under the mats and answering back. The day to go to confession came. I went wondering what to expect. It was not all all frightening as I had anticipated. I was asked whether I intended to try and avoid doing these things again. I said I did, and now something has happened which made me think there was something in it after all. As I went away from that box I suddenly felt pure. Now it wasn't because I really believed in what I had just done but for the first and only time, I felt as if all my past had been wiped out. I went back resolved to try not to upset the older of the two people. We were told to call her ma'am. I really did try after that and the year I was there went very quickly.

I was told that as I was a fairly tall girl, I should become a parlour maid, so I waited at the table, cleaned the silver and did the drawing room. None of the work we did could really be called training. Monday was wash day. We all worked as a team, some washing, some mangling and others hanging out. Afterwards we had what was called Panyan dinner. This was everything left over in the safe. It all went into a stew and often one would find a bit of jam tart or apple pie in the stew. Tuesday was baking day. Matron did the baking and no-one was allowed to help her, only with the washing up or fetching and carrying. There was one girl who would have loved to do cooking, but that didn't come into the training.

I was introduced to a new form of cooking while was there, Hay Box cookery. This was a wooden box lined with layers and layers of newspaper, then inside that a layer of hay flannel. In this we would put our porridge after it had been first brought to the boil. It was then wrapped in another piece of blanket and put in the hay box overnight. Stews could also be kept simmering in this way. It saved a lot of money for fuel, as we had porridge every day.

The war was over before I went there, but food and fuel were in short supply. The peace night celebrations happened in an allotment opposite to us in Buckland Hill, while the fireworks were let off at the top of a newly built Tilling Stevens factory. These were beautiful. I had never seen anything like them before but it was spoiled for me because I was terrified of the bangs. I always have been. While all the others were going into raptures I was trembling in the background. The whole evening was just moments of pure terror for me and no-one could understand me. I can't myself, even a burst balloon sends me into shivers.

On Sunday, after dinner, we had a free period when we could write one letter only. I wanted to write to Auntie Bea, Aunt Bishop and my mother, so I wrote to Auntie Bea enclosing one for my mother as I knew she would take it down to her. The letter had to do duty to both Aunts. We had no pocket money at all and as I think about it, I would have thought that training would include managing money so that we would go out in the world with an idea of how to get on. When I did get the very first month's money, one pound, I needed a new pair of shoes for indoors, as I was walking around with my shoes falling off my feet, till my employer saw and bought me a pair which I had to pay back in three instalments. After that she gave a little oversight to my spending which was good of her, even if I didn't appreciate it at the time.

Our letters were always opened before we had them. I used to look forward to these letters containing all the news of home. I would be very homesick afterwards. One very funny thing happened. One girl's parents had a small farm and sent the pigs' chitterlings to the girl. The look of disgust and horror had to be seen to be believed. It seemed the girl particularly loved these chitterlings and promptly burst into tears when they were thrown away. I must admit they did look revolting, but quite a few said how nice they were, so no doubt they tasted better than they looked.

Christmas came. I must say they did try to make us get into the spirit. A corner of the room was curtained off and all sorts of parcels were put behind. All the parcels from outside were put there as well. We all had to wait until Christmas day for what we might have been sent. After church and dinner we all collected in the drawing room and Ma'am handed out the presents in rotation. One girl, Sarah, had far more than anyone else, so Ma'am said she should not have them all in one day. I thought this was very unfair. After all we were not babies to be jealous of someone else's good fortune. The poor girl was upset too and was very rude to Ma'am, so in the end the girl was sent to do penance in the chapel. I think they were wrong to withhold her presents, but there was nothing we could do about it. Our Christmas was spoiled as well because we kept thinking about Sarah up in the cold chapel.

One of our punishments was to go to the chapel and do penance. Some of us did, but one girl was seen by Matron hanging out of the window talking to some workmen in the allotments opposite. Now it was a funny thing but we were all supposed to be as bad as the one who had committed a particular offence. We were all punished for this girl's behaviour, although most of us wouldn't have thought of doing anything of that nature. No-one was allowed to go out for a week except to go to church, or to work. I was one of these workers, who went to a house in London Road twice a week. I had to do anything that the cook or parlour maid asked me, from chopping the wood for cook's fire to polishing the floor when the parlour maid had done the room. This was another way of learning to work. I didn't learn much except how to talk about my employer behind her back. They did a lot of that over dinner. We had far better food there than we did at the home, so I enjoyed the work. I got the odd sweet or cake as well. One girl had to leave very early after dinner, so she had hers without waiting for us. We were waiting to be served with our pudding. It looked delicious – a chocolate blancmange. The girl had hers. We couldn't understand it. She was getting slower and slower eating her portion. Then when we had ours we found out it had been made without sugar. It really did want some getting down. Matron said 'get on with it, we are all eating the same'. They were eating theirs without any fuss. When the girl who cleared the table came back, she whispered that she had scraped the dish which their pudding had come from and theirs had got sugar in. We felt that was mean. If there wasn't enough sugar they could have made some sort of pudding that didn't need so much or at least told us there wasn't enough. We were treated like children and resented it.

I had at least got away from the stigma of having no father. Three other girls were in the same boat, so it was a subject avoided. One girl had a father in prison or he had been. We were quite a nice bunch of girls though all had something in our past which we would rather not talk about. I have never seen one of them since the day I left. One went to work daily and was so useful that they asked if she might stay with them permanently. A few days later she went there and I would see her about the town while I remained in Maidstone.

I wasn't a good worker. I needed quite a bit of taking in hand. Neither the training I got at the home nor the training I had at Aunt's fitted me for work. I knew little of what was in store for me and was looking forward to going into service, the day of which was ever getting closer. Then I was told that a place had been found for me at Eastbourne. I was to be a kitchen maid and I had been trained, if that is the word, as a parlour maid. It was April when I went on the train with Ma'am to the boarding house to start work.

Chapter 9

MY FIRST JOB AT EASTBOURNE

It was a new beginning all round. I had never been on a train, so the whole journey was a source of interest. Ma'am sat opposite me trying to instil in me a sense of responsibility. What a pity it had not been said before, for with all the excitement of seeing what was going on around me, plus the little twinges of alarm when I thought about what I was going to find when I arrived, most of what she said passed over my head.

I saw quite a different side of Ma'am's character from that which we saw in the home. After talking to me about my future she just went to sleep and I saw her as she really was, a quite old lady trying to hang on to her life's work. Perhaps there was not a pension at that time. I did not know, but certainly she never did anything towards the training in the home except be there. Most Matrons would not have taken on all the responsibility as that one did.

We arrived in Eastbourne and went in a taxi to the boarding house which was on the sea front not far from the Grand Hotel and at the foot of the cliffs, Beachy Head. I was taken to the little sitting room at the back of the house and introduced to my employers, two of them, sisters, as I found out later. I was to receive thirteen pounds a year, paid monthly. Half of this I was to send by postal order to the home for my outfit. I could earn a shilling a week extra if I was willing to do a bit in the garden at the back of the house. This I was glad to do, because I had no money at all for a month, not even a stamp to write to my Aunt, and I liked gardening.

I was to have Thursday afternoon off when I had done the washing up. That would depend on how soon the guests wanted to go out. I soon got a routine going about that. I would wash up all the saucepans as I went, if I wasn't called away that was, then I would go up and listen at the door of the room I wanted to clear to see if I could hear them talking. If not I would go in. More often than not they had gone out and forgotten to ring the bell which was one of their rules. I lost all one afternoon's outing through that. There was another girl three years older than me who did the bedrooms, while my job was to clean the kitchen, light the fires, do my employers' sitting room and then take up their morning tea. By then it was time to cook breakfast. Guests brought their own food and we cooked it. It was a peculiar arrangement between the guests and management really because we in the kitchen had all the food left, so we lived very well. On Saturday we all set to cleaning the rooms ready for the new guests and helping to take out cases of the departing guests. My employer was very strict that both should have equal chances for any tips we were to have. It was these tips and the one shilling a week for keeping the garden tidy that was to be my pocket money. There would not be any in the winter, so I had decided to pay my outfit money in three goes instead of six. I got enough tips in that first month to buy a new

Beachy Head Lighthouse.

pair of shoes. I only bought cheap ones and before the month was out they were worn out. They cost me exactly the same as one month's wages. I had been there three months and had paid off my outfit, so at last all money I had was free.

Our employers were quite good to us. We got grumbled at if we were lazy or did not do our work properly, but that was to be expected and was our own fault. I was really happy there. Only one thing marred my life. I did so want to go and see my aunts and my mother. I had no day off or I could have gone home and back. The other girl said we would have a week's holiday when we had been there a year, but that meant two whole years without seeing them. I think if I had told my employers how I felt they would have let me go, but I did not like to. I had been ordered about too long to be able to ask for or to suggest anything for myself. In a way, everything that happened to me was my own fault, for if I could only have risen above my fear of doing wrong, and asked for what I wanted, I am sure I could have gone home for a day and come back the better for it.

Beatie, the other girl, used to sneak out after we had gone to bed at night. I was much too tired. The day was very long for me as we rose at six, and it was really hard going to get it all done before breakfast time came round. The evening meals were never over until ten, at least by the time we had washed up. Beatie did the cutlery in her little kitchen while I did mine in the main one. Our bedroom was by the backdoor on the ground floor, so it was easy for Beatie to go out. Of course I never told on her, but somehow our boss found out. I think it was one of the guests taking a late night stroll who saw her and in conversation with our employer she brought the subject up. Beatie was furious as she thought I had given her away, but was soon told who it was. I got in the wrong as well for knowing it was going on and not saying anything.

Grand Parade, Eastbourne, about 1920.

Beatie gave a month's notice and left at the end of that time. I had my first full month's wages that month, as up to then I had been paying for my outfit of clothes. I should have bought a pair of shoes with it which would have taken the whole amount. Instead I got a pair that had been left by one of the guests and made do with those. It was understood that anything left by the guests of that nature was ours; usually they weren't much good, but they did a turn. The shoes were too big being size 6 and I took 5 at that time, but I slopped about quite happily in them as I had spent all my money on a sea-plane ride. It had come to Eastbourne for one week before going to some other place. The fare was one pound. I had looked out every time I heard it go overhead. We didn't see many planes in those days. On Thursday I hurried to the place where it started with the intention of just watching. When the man came along and said 'just got room for one', I found myself inside and away we went. It was worth every penny. The ground seemed like a small garden and people looked like beetles. We went over the sea then inland for a bit and it was all over and I had a whole month to wait for my next wage.

I didn't dare say what I had done and I myself knew it was very foolish, but I did still have my shilling a week to rely on. Fortunately the shoes I had from the guest were a strong pair, stronger than I had been buying, and although they were too big, they lasted well. I think I learned a lesson or two in fact. One, to think before I squandered and two, to buy shoes that would last. I was very heavy on shoes. I did a lot of kneeling about and that is very bad on shoes. All these things should have been part of my training but I had to learn the hard way. I always learned by my mistakes though.

I was really happy there and I was treated well, except for the fact that I still felt insecure and the longing to go home to Tenterden was becoming a mania with me. Oh, if only I had plucked up the courage to say how I felt, what a lot of heartache I would have saved myself, but I dared not.

I liked my work. I loved the sea and I had a bathing costume left by one of the guests. One was allowed to go bathing on the beach without changing in a hut before six o'clock, but it was a byelaw that bathing suits must be changed in a hut after that time. My employer said 'Why not go out before work and have a swim?' so I set the alarm for half past five and would go out before work. I enjoyed that. There were two or three other girls from the houses around out as well, and we would have a lovely time.

I had taken my month's wages when the idea came to get on a train and go home. I thought I could be back in time for bed and no-one need know. I was so innocent: I just did not stop to think how long it would take, but took a train to Tenterden, only to be told by the stationmaster that it would only go as far as Ashford, where I would have to change. This I did, finally arriving at Ashford at eight o'clock. When I asked for a ticket to Tenterden I was told there were no more trains that day. I was stumped. I had never had to manage anything myself, so I just stood feeling like bursting into tears any moment, which no doubt I would have done had it not been for a woman who said 'come along deary, I think there is a bus'. We hurried into the town and there was. It was in the yard all ready to go. I was so overwrought that I kissed the woman and boarded the bus. My troubles were not over though, as I was to find out later. As I got nearer to Tenterden I began to get excited, and at St Michael's, there through the trees I got my first glimpse of the church. There was a lump in my throat. I really was going home at last. What ever trouble I got into when I got back was worth it as I rounded the last corner and was in the High Street. I passed the house where Aunt used to live, but she had recently moved to a house lower down in the town. I got off the bus and hurried to find my dear old Aunt Bea and Uncle, but, when I got there they were out. It seemed such a stalemate after all my excitement that I couldn't wait for them to come home but went off to see the other aunt in the meantime. Aunt was very surprised to see me. I told them I had come home to see them. When I said I must go back first thing in the morning they said I had run away. It wasn't any good what I said. They said I had run away and was just telling lies. Uncle disappeared and came back with the woman who had been responsible for my welfare when I lived with the two aunts. I repeated that I had not run away and was returning in the morning. It was no use, they would not let me go to Auntie Bea as I had intended, neither would they allow me to send a telegram to say where I was. I was forced to go with the

'I rounded the last corner and was in the High Street'.

woman down to the Union. I was by now stunned and in despair. I was like a prisoner. I couldn't see that I had done anything very wrong. Foolish yes, but not wrong. The bell at the house was rung and a Matron came to the door. I was now beyond anything. I could not speak. I just stood there dumb while they talked about what I was supposed to have done.

I was taken in to what I found out was the receiving ward. The officer on duty made me undress, my hair was combed with a tooth comb, I was bathed and horrible print clothes, two sizes too big, were given to me. I was not allowed to dress but taken over to the infirmary and put to bed. The woman next to me was dying of cancer, it was terrible. Every time she drew a breath she screamed. Some woman the other side kept saying 'shut up' to her, but the poor woman kept on and on.

The next morning a bell went and I had to get up. I was sent to the dining room to eat my breakfast. I went with the other women and sat on a form. In front of me there was a thick slice of bread with a square of margarine on it and a big chipped mug of blackish looking tea. I couldn't eat anything, but I drank a little tea. I could see mother the other side of the room, but no-one was allowed to speak. After grace, I had to go back to the infirmary, and I did not see my mother until the Saturday.

I was dreading going to bed, but I had to when the bell went. The woman was still screaming. I heard her at intervals all day. Our life in there was ruled by the bell – to get up – to go to breakfast – to go to work. I was helping in the infirmary with the old people. Then bells again for dinner, work again, then leave off

The courtyard at the Union.

time, tea and bed. I was allowed to chat with the other inmates in the evening, but we were not allowed outside the ward. The doors were locked, although the door that led to the lavatories in the yard was open, but we could not go anywhere from there. We were surrounded by a wall.

One woman I did know, Fan, who had looked after me as a little girl. She helped make my life a bit more bearable. On the third day the woman died. I woke up to find a lot of bustle going on in the bed next to me. I put up my head

A corner of Tenterden unchanged since 1920.

and was promptly told to go to sleep — as if I could, with a dead woman in the bed next to me. I was glad she had died, but I could hear that screaming for a long time afterwards.

On Saturday, my mother came over to see me. Somehow I couldn't think of anything to say. I had been sending her an odd stamp or two, so she would miss all that. On Monday I was asked to go and stand in the front hall. I was not told why but that was nothing unusual. No-one was told anything. We were treated as prisoners. In fact we were worse off. At least they knew what length of time they had to serve, while I knew nothing. I stood in the hall for about half an hour, then a woman came out of a side room, and would you believe it, it was the vicar's daughter. I said I wanted to go back to my job, but I was told that I would not be allowed to go back even if they would have me. I had to behave myself or I would remain where I was for the rest of my life. That woman still brought out the worst in me. I then had to go to the cutting room to see the Matron who took back the clothes I had been given when I was admitted and gave me some which were a better fit. I was given a number which was sewn into everything I wore, even the stockings. I had to wear a flannel sort of vest. It was more like a shirt and it pricked terribly. The worst things were the knickers. They were a band of calico with two legs joined on at the waist, but open half way down, then joined at the bottom of the knickers to make a leg. I hated those things. They weren't decent. It's a good thing we had long frocks. The number of my frock showed through on the right side, not much but enough to make me feel that I was a prisoner indeed.

My dear old Auntie Bea came to see me. She had asked for me to go with her and arrange to go back to my old job. It appeared that she had written to them. They had said I could go if I wished to but the Board of Guardians would not allow it. They, and they alone, must decide what my future was to be. It was pointed out that they had paid for my keep since I was three years old, and I had been born at their expense. This of course was true. Auntie Bea was left in no doubt that she had no say in my future.

Every Wednesday was visiting day for outside visitors, and every Wednesday and Sunday without fail she came to see me, even when she went hop picking she would come down in the evening to bring the little luxuries, like cake, biscuits or sweets. She couldn't see me of course, but she left them for me. I think she was my saviour in those dreadful few weeks, for at times the feeling of despair was so great that all I could think about was the fact that I was there and perhaps I would be for the rest of my life, like my mother and most of the other inmates who all seemed to have been there for a long time.

The members of the Board of Guardians were all quite good local people, but the whole set up was wrong. Whatever they may have thought of me privately, there was no show of common humanity. No little talk to see why I had behaved as they thought I had. They were told that I had run away, and that was what they believed. I needed correcting and they were the ones to do it. My feelings had nothing to do with it. I was to them a chattel to be disposed as they thought fit. Perhaps I am wrong in thinking all this but that's how it seemed to me. Certainly there was no show of feeling, either from the Board or the Officers. Reform in this sort of thing has gone a long way since that time, but how many women have been turned into human cabbages, through a system which saw only the fault and never the cause. The ability to think for themselves and to make a decision was gradually taken out of them. I could see this process in its various stages in the other inmates around me, not that I realised it at the time, but I can see it now, looking back. We weren't classed as people, we were male or female inmates. I had just begun to live a different life, where I was taken at my face value, but now I had come to this.

On Saturdays I was allowed to go out for a walk. I did go out the first week, but we went through the town and I saw someone I knew; she was a girl from my school days. She straight away went and bought me a packet of sweets. I was so ashamed. I was wearing a black straw boater hat. It looked really ugly and with my grey shabby coat I felt and looked a sight. I tried to get out of going out after that but the rule was that we had to unless we were ill. It was a privilege I was told. I should appreciate it. It was also held as a punishment over us. 'If you don't behave you will not be allowed out on Saturday' we were frequently told.

After three months, I was told that I was to be sent to another place. If I ran away from that, I would be kept in the Union for the rest of my life.

Chapter 10

IN SERVICE

The new job was at Iden, near Rye, and I was there for a three months trial. It was winter time, so the roads between there and Tenterden would often be impassable for buses, owing to the flooded roads. It was agreed that if I was suitable, I could go for a weekend to stay with my Auntie Bea if I wished. Perhaps after all they had believed me when I said I had just come home to see her and not run away. I was to get fifteen shillings a month while I was being trained. It was a farmhouse and there was a great deal of work to do. The son and daughter did the farm work with the aid of one man, while another son, who was crippled and also a little retarded mentally, helped the elderly mother to run the house.

They were very nice to me, but somehow I never came up to their expectations. I had to get used to farm life, to unsettled hours, to cleaning round sick animals by the kitchen fire. If the daughter could have been at home to show me the responsibilities and the ropes, I know I would have been able to cope, but the mother would worry me, always enquiring what I was doing. I didn't have a chance. I know I would have loved the farm life, but it had been impressed on the old lady that I must be made to do things right. She fussed and I got confused, and at the end I knew I wouldn't suit and I didn't. The daughter was so nice to me and said I was not suitable and a more experienced girl was needed. The thought of being sent back to that place again was too much. I would get a job and leave. Once again I left, but this time ran away.

I should have known better. I just did not stop to think but set off very early in the morning to walk to Tenterden. It was a waste of time, for I was just overtaken by the daughter and taken back. She was very upset as she had been kind to me and could not understand why I should want to leave.

The fact remained, I had always had hanging over my head 'you must behave, for if you are brought back again, you may be here for life.' Why couldn't those in charge of my welfare realise how it was affecting me and say 'If you do not suit them we will find you somewhere else'. They knew by now that I had suited them at Eastbourne and they did know about the farmer. It could have been avoided. Meanwhile the trouble I was in was having a very bad effect on me. I was getting the feeling that everyone was against me. Actually both the Board of Guardians and Matron were doing their best. It was a matter of lack of communication.

So here I was once again, back in the one place more than any other that I hated. This time I was sent to the main part of the building. My mother was sorry to see me again as she had a letter from me only a few days before and I had said nothing about coming back.

The Union at Tenterden is now a geriatric hospital.

I went to sleep with a lot of other women, about fourteen in one ward. At night we were locked in. Anyone wishing to use the toilet had a commode, as there were many quite old people in the ward. There was a terrible smell by morning. The last person to use the commode had to empty it, so no-one used it towards morning unless it was absolutely vital.

I was sent to the laundry to work. It was very hard, from eight till five. There was no pay at all. We were all earning our keep, we were told. My job was in the washhouse. I stood at a tub, one of six in a row. All I did was to scrub and scrub clothes, shirts one time, dresses another, underclothes another. Each had their special day for cleaning. I was enveloped in a huge coarse apron and a big piece of rubber to keep me dry, which it didn't. I got wet above and below the rubber bit. Each evening we all went in soaked to the skin. In summer, we would stay out in the sun and steam dry. In winter we would try and get as near the ward fire as possible to dry out. It just depended on how heavy handed the women who did the sewing had been during the day. We had one large scuttle of coal a day, so if they had been too heavy handed in the daytime, then there was no fire for the evening. The only thing to do then was to go to bed after tea. There was no rule to say that we could not. Our hands were wrinkled with being in the water all day.

It really is amazing how one comes to accept life as one finds it. I got into the routine of five and a half days work, then Saturday afternoon outing. I loved it best if we went across the fields. There I was not so likely to meet anyone I knew.

High Halden Church.

Less than three months later I was again found a place, this time at High Halden, with two elderly ladies. It was a beautiful house, something like an old rectory, standing in a large garden and grounds. Opposite the kitchen window was a small lake on which were moorhens and ducks. My first impression was that I would love this place and I was determined never, ever to go back again to the Union. Auntie Bea found out that if I stayed till I was eighteen, I could then leave if I wanted to. I was to have twelve pounds a year, which would go up to thirteen pounds after I had been there a year. I could go out to church on Sunday evenings and during the summer I could stay out till 8.30 p.m. but in the winter must come straight home after church. I could have a day off once a month to go home to Auntie Bea. I soon found out that a day out meant after dinner and I had to be home before dark. I had to walk both ways to Tenterden so there wasn't much time when I did get there. I looked forward to those days.

The work wasn't hard but it never ended. When I had done what I was set to do, then I was found a job in the garden, so my whole day was taken up. I had very little time to read or mend my clothes. In the winter I did have a little while to read, but there was only the daily paper and at weekends the children's newspaper. I got it when it was about three weeks old, but not to worry. On the day that it was delivered, I would be round the porch cleaning the steps. They got a quick slosh with the flannel then I would read the instalment. It was very exciting being about Martians who were saving Britain from a poison gas. It was very far fetched for that time, but I just lapped it up.

I think those two ladies were the meanest people I had ever known. Each week my food, such as jam and margarine, was doled out. I had a little dish of jam, usually gooseberry. This was watered down as it was said to be jam essence. Sometimes the gardener would catch a rabbit. Then they would have the body and legs, while I was given the head with an onion and some potatoes. I was told that the head was the best part because it contained the brains which were so nutritious. That may be the case, but it wasn't very filling.

At the end of the month, I would be called into the study to receive my wages, less stoppages. I was stopped one penny for each time I dropped a spoon or fork, as it lost a pennyworth of silver every time it was dropped, so they said. Then the younger of the two would nearly always have some cast off clothes of hers which she would sell me. Some of these were really old-fashioned, but I just agreed as I would not give them anything to find fault with.

The things I put up with during those two years nobody knows. I was very unhappy, just the one day to look forward to. Dear old Auntie Bea would fuss over me. It was the highlight of the month.

Uncle was getting very feeble. He hardly went out at all. His mental faculties were still very alert, however, and I had many a chat with him about things not being as they were in his younger days. His mother had sometimes to make a meal for the family of five from swedes which he got from a farmer. Poor man, he often went to bed hungry, so things were improving all the time. We did have enough to eat, even if it was of poor quality.

Auntie Bea would walk back with me, at least as far as St Michael's, so the journey wasn't as lonely as it could have been.

The first year went by, but they kept putting off paying me the promised rise. In the end I was forced to ask them for more money. They could not have been more incensed. It was the height of bad manners, I was told, to ask for a rise, especially as they were so good to me, giving me clothes etc. Well the clothes were cast-offs and I had to pay something for them. I was determined not to make a fuss about it. I could wait until I was eighteen, when I could leave. I felt as if the time would never come.

The fashion had just come in to have a fringe, and when home one month, I cut mine. I thought it looked very nice, but no sooner had I done it than I became very frightened. I was sure it wasn't going to go down very well with the two ladies, and I was right. The elder lady gave one look at me when I took in the supper that night and let out a scream. 'You look a sight' she said. The other one looked round and told me to pull my cap down over the fringe until it grew. So I wore it right down on my brow. I looked a worse sight like that, but if that's what they wanted, well I wasn't going to upset them if I could help it. I was a few months off eighteen by now, and I could afford to wait.

On the day of my birthday, Auntie sent me a letter. 'Thank God my darling, you are free' she said. Free I thought I was, and I found myself humming as I went about my work. When the end of the month came around I went into the study as usual and waited for my employer to come in, as was usual each afternoon, to give me orders for the next day and also to give me my month's wages.

I felt a bit frightened as I told her that I wished to give in a month's notice, but got over it somehow and was surprised to note how well she received it. I was not questioned as to why I wished to leave, nor what I intended to do. It was over, or so I thought as I went back to the kitchen to carry on with my duties. I was prepared for a nasty time for the next month, but I could put up with that.

The following day I was sent into the kitchen after dinner and told to clean the silver before I went up to my room to change. This was very odd as I had cleaned it earlier in the week, but no doubt I would have a lot of extra jobs to do now, I thought. I had nearly finished the work when the door opened and in came the Matron from the Union. 'Come along Dorothy' she said. I just stood there and looked at her. I had no idea what she meant. 'Come along' she said, 'You have been giving your employers a lot of trouble, now you must come back to the house.' I was dumbfounded. I just could not grasp it. My trunk was in the hall which was why I had been kept in the kitchen. They bundled me into the taxi and I was taken back again to that dreaded house. I went through the usual drill and was put into a ward with the sewing women. I could do nothing. I was in a state of shock.

Chapter 11

BACK TO THE WORKHOUSE

The following day I was ill and was transferred to the infirmary. When the doctor called, I was examined. He was my old doctor from my childhood days. He asked a lot of questions about the people I had worked for and what had brought about my return to the Union. I was in a state, I know. I was suddenly overcome with the feeling that I would never again be outside, that I never, never would be free to decide my own future. I broke down and cried until I was too weak to cry any more.

Meanwhile, the doctor was writing things down. He told me to do what I could to carry out what I was asked to do, to behave myself. He would give me some medicine which would help me. 'You have some friends, just pin your faith in them. Somehow I did feel better after that and a few days later I was sent into the kitchen to work and sent back to the main block to live.

The women were rather pleased about it of course. They couldn't be blamed really. After all they were there for life, or so it appeared, as they had been placed under the Board of Control. I don't quite know what the function of this board was. What I did know was that people who were considered to be below par mentally, or some who had behave unruly or come before a court, were brought there.

Every so often certain people would come and see new inmates. If they did not come up to a certain standard, they were certified and became known as under the Board of Control. A lot of them were already certified, a few were there because they were homeless. The day these people came was known by the inmates as 'the day the gentlemen call'.

I was to be examined the next day they came, and with great glee the women told me I would be sure to be certified as I had been given three chances to stay in a job and no-one would keep me. That wasn't true as I would still have been in the job at High Halden if I had been willing to stay and put up with the way I was treated. I had been satisfactory all the time I had been there. It was only when I tried to leave that they trumped up the charge that I was unsuitable.

It was some three weeks later when Matron told me to put on my best dress the next day, and to carry on with my normal work but to be careful not to get wet as I was to be seen by the Board when they came.

Everyone was whispering about the gentlemen coming. It was all right for them, they had not got to be seen, only me. I had seen the doctor again and had been told not to worry and to carry on normally. How could I help worrying when it was my future they were going to decide. The doctor said that they were trying to have me certified, but he had known me since I was a child and he knew my school record, and he also knew I was as sane as he was, so his advice

The former laundry at Tenterden Union.

to me was to speak up, and try to answer all questions intelligently. 'Don't be afraid of the man' he said 'and you will be all right'. I shall always be thankful for the advice the doctor gave me, for in my state of mind I was likely to have answered just yes or no and left it at that.

I put on my Sunday dress in the morning, and went to work as usual in the laundry. Now our laundry was a long narrow room with wooden troughs one side at which some of us stood from eight to twelve scrubbing clothes, one day underclothes, sometimes men's filthy corduroys, or even worse, men's red handkerchiefs. There were two coppers in the wash room which were looked after by a little woman who was quite a character. One day when she had been upset by the laundress she suddenly jumped up on the ledge between the coppers and threatened to jump into the boiling water. The other women were screaming, but she had done the same thing a good many times before, so the laundress just told her to get down and stop clowning around. This time the woman did not, but leaned over the copper till it looked as if she would fall in. All of us started to scream. We were afraid that if we went towards her, she would jump in sheer bravado. Suddenly, a man appeared as if by magic, crept up behind her and pulled her off the copper. It was a tense moment, and but for the timely appearance of the man from the infirmary department, who had come in by a different door and so was out of sight of the woman on the copper, might have ended tragically. We never saw her in the laundry again, thank goodness.

On this particular day that I had to meet the Board, I was put in charge of the coppers, so that I would not get too wet or dirty before the gentlemen came.

The reason for being interviewed in my place of work was so that I would be as normal as possible, though how anyone could be feeling normal when all around people were saying 'don't get dirty, don't get wet, be quiet, the gentlemen will soon be here and they will hear you' I don't know. The whole atmosphere was one of excitement, or fear in my case. The morning dragged on until at eleven o'clock I was called to stand in the front hall. A woman came out to talk to me. She was the wife of a local tradesman. I had known her all my life. She was wearing a large bunch of artificial violets in her coat. 'Smell my violets, Dorothy' she said. Now I wouldn't have dared to have said that they were artificial in the ordinary way, but the words of the doctor came back to me and I realised what he meant. I smelled the flowers, 'yes' I said, 'they get them up as good as real nowadays, don't they?' I was overcome with boldness as soon as I said it, but it seemed to go down all right, for she smiled and went back to the office. Other men and women came out, looked at me but never spoke. Then I was sent back to the laundry to await the rest, still told not to get dirty. What I had said to the woman in the hall had brought back my confidence. I was no longer afraid and would be ready for whatever they asked me. To my dying day I will be grateful to my doctor for his advice. I wouldn't have dreamed of answering as I did without it.

Presently the great moment arrived. There was great excitement in the laundry. They hadn't to meet them, so they could enjoy to the full what was to happen to me, and they did.

I was called out to the ironing room where I was alone with the two men. The first one smiled at me and I must admit he managed to put me at ease. The other one just stood back listening. I was asked why I had left three jobs. It was evident that they did not know how I came to leave High Halden. I explained how I thought I was free to give in my notice. I had been there two years and was then eighteen. This man was extremely nice to me and I was feeling that it would be all right after all, when without warning the man at the back suddenly barked – that was the only way to describe the way he spoke to me – 'What is the difference between dark and light?' I nearly came to grief over this, for I was taken by surprise and I began to stutter – 'We can see in the light' I said 'but not so well in the dark'. Then my confidence returned. I went on to say how the sun and moon had some bearing on the light and the dark. It was my favourite lesson at school so I warmed to the subject.

He wrote something in a book. Whether it went down well or not, I couldn't say. Suddenly he barked again 'What is the difference between an apple and an orange?' This was easy. I was now quite at ease as I went into the difference of skin texture, juice etc. This was another favourite of mine at school. I hoped they would not ask me where the oranges come from. That was not a good subject. The third question was quite matter of fact. I think by then I had made the grade, for he smiled at me and asked what was the difference between glass and

Dorothy as a teenager.

wood. I went on to talk about the manufacture of furniture from wood; how after the tree had been cut down it went through various treatments to make it more suitable and to preserve the wood. He said 'you'll do'. Then they both shook hands with me and went out.

I went back to the washhouse. It must have taken more out of me than I thought because I could hardly walk. The laundress told me to go and change my dress for my work one, then to stay out of sight until dinner time. I went to the dormitory and the woman there was all agog to know how I got on. She was telling me where I might be sent. I know she was enjoying every minute of it. After all they had so little variety in their lives. I just broke down and cried. It seemed that nothing would stop me being kept in that place for the rest of my life. I was in the deepest despair that day.

I heard nothing for a long time. Then a new girl came into the house. Her mother had signed for her to be put into the place for correction for two years. She had a little girl, who had been adopted as soon as she had been born. Her mother said she would not allow her to keep it, but she signed the girl away all the same. It appeared that Marion, the girl, had been going to the soldiers' camps at night and had in fact become a prostitute. Her mother took the money which she made by it and it wasn't until the girl had the baby that she made any fuss about it. Poor Marion, she was more sinned against than sinning. Her mother knew what she was doing so could have stopped her if she had so wished. We palled up right away. She was five years older than I was, but it was nice to have someone young enough to talk to. I realised that she was not a good girl, but at least we were more of an age and had more in common than most women had in there.

It was the custom for the women to sit on the bed of their special friend each evening till they heard the officer on duty come along to lock the bedroom door. This meant coming along a stone corridor and it was well nigh impossible to come along without being heard, so although it was against the rules to be out of bed after eight, well, we all did it. This night Marion was sitting on my bed trying to show me where I was going wrong in a knitting pattern I was doing. I suddenly noticed that all the other women were in bed. In fact none of them had been out of their beds all evening. I was just about to say to the two friends opposite 'why are you so early in bed tonight?' when the door opened and in came Matron. It was obvious to us by now that the others knew she was coming and the fact that Matron had crept down the corridor meant only one thing, someone had told on us. It had to be someone who saw the Matron. The only ones were the two opposite. They both worked for the Matron and they were both safely tucked up in bed that night, though why they should do it to us when they themselves were out of bed on other nights was beyond me. Well, we got a right ticking off, but the next day, more was to follow.

As it was a Saturday, there was no work after twelve o'clock. We were all in the day room when in walked Matron. We were quite expecting another dressing-down, so we stood in front of her. Then, turning to the other women in the room, she said, 'Stand back from these two, keep clear. They pollute the very air you breathe.' I was astounded. I had done nothing more than break a rule which we all did. I just could not understand what all the fuss was about. I was prepared to be punished for breaking a rule. After all we knew the risk we ran if we disobeyed an order, but what Matron was saying was something quite different. I had until then led a very sheltered life, always being in service or in the Union itself. All the seamy part of life was over my head.

I was asked to go to see the master after that. Now he was quite different. He told me that Matron was very worried in case I became a bad girl as Marion was. He told me she was a street girl and not a good companion for me. He went on to say that I would be going out one day so I must behave myself. I suppose Matron was really only trying to protect me from the influence of a bad girl, but I think it was a very wicked thing to say to anyone at all. Of course, I shall never know what Matron's informant had actually said to her, so I suppose it was best to say nothing, especially since now, at last, I had news that I was going out again.

When I returned to the day room, Marion was gone. She had been transferred to the infirmary to work, so I seldom saw her. Soon after this I was called to the hall again. There was a farmer's wife who needed a maid. Her former maid had left in a hurry and as the lady had just had a baby, she needed a maid at once.

New House Farm.

My future mistress went into all the details with me – the times I would have off, and so on. I knew I was going to like this place. I saw the vicar's daughter again before I left, and this time I asked when I would be able to move without asking the permission of the Board of Guardians. I was told to stay there until I was twenty-one. If by then I was giving satisfaction, then I could do as I wished. So now I knew, but I felt in my bones that I would get on with the farmer and his wife.

Chapter 12

HAPPINESS AT NEW HOUSE FARM

The first thing my new employer did was to help me to get a decent outfit of clothes together. My mistress made over some of her own to fit me, as the clothes I came out with were old fashioned to say the least. Gradually, over the months, I built up a nice wardrobe. I could now hold up my head with the rest of the world. Only those who have experienced the same feeling of inferiority as I had could begin to understand the difference it made to me to be dressed as other girls were, or to be able to talk about what I intended to do on my time off. I was making my own decisions at last and it was a grand feeling. Before I had been there long, the children were coming out to me for meals; they had exactly the same in the dining room as I did in the kitchen. They were very fond of me and I of them.

I was nineteen when I went to them and I stayed there four years, four happy years. Then I felt I must get away to start in some work that had no link at all with the Union. My mistress, even one who had been as good to me as she had, would not have understood even if I had tried to explain. I had to leave and get a place for myself, with no help from the Board of Guardians. There was still a nagging feeling that I just might be dragged back to that dreadful workhouse. Until I had cut all ties, I could not feel absolutely free.

I was sorry, for I had been very happy with my employer. The children were real darlings, the smallest one being only a few weeks old when I went there. I had come to love them almost as my own. I did a lot for them – took them out, met them from school, played games with them, bathed them – they even had their meals with me, except for breakfast, as I had so much to get on with while the family had breakfast.

I was treated as one of the family. I had a sweet when they did, ate the same as them and in every way was treated kindly. I was allowed to go to a dance, but I didn't fit in. I hadn't grown into adult life gradually as the other girls. I felt awkward and gauche and was certainly 'one of the wallflowers'. I did join a folk dance club, and found this more to my liking. I had a regular holiday and went to stay with a friend at Dartford who had known me through Auntie Bea's sister and kept up an irregular correspondence with me at Christmas, and on birthdays.

The farmhouse was a very long way from town and down a very lonely lane. At one time there was a scare that a 'gorilla' man with one arm longer than the other was lurking about. Going home one evening I could see through the moonlight, which made dazzled patches of dark and light on the lane, what looked exactly like a man with one long arm. I was too near to run back and anyhow I had to pass him to get home, so I rushed past him, stumbled over a stone and fell headlong. He came to see if I was hurt, but I was so petrified I just scrambled by

A Kentish lane.

The oasthouse at New House Farm as it is today.

on hands and knees. Then he spoke, and it was a man I knew who lived in one of the cottages nearby. He had a mackintosh over his arm, which to my frightened way of thinking was the long arm of a gorilla man. My knees were bleeding, my stockings and dress were torn to bits on the rough gravel all for nothing, but it is an eerie thing to walk home in the dark.

The work at the farm was very different from what I was to go to after I left. At the farm there were certain days for certain jobs, and certain things which had to be done daily, such as washing up the separator, drying it and fixing it ready for use the next day. Monday was washday, all by hand, which the farmer's wife did. I did my own afterwards. Tuesday was bedrooms, and so on through the week. I always finished before midday meal and in the afternoon I could go out on my own or with the children. I preferred to take the baby out and meet the others from school. I did a lot of catching up with my childhood, playing with those three. Perhaps that is why I went down so well with them. I would have been quite happy to remain there with them until I was married but, as they said, 'I had to leave' and so I did.

Chapter 13

INDEPENDENCE AT LAST

After leaving New House Farm I went to stay with relatives of Uncle Ambrose at Dartford. They had an adopted daughter of about my own age, and the two of us sought work through an employment agency at Bexley. We were found a series of temporary jobs, which meant that I saw quite a bit of variety.

The first job was in a house in Erith. By the standards of that day, the house was modern to the extreme. The master of the house was something in electrics, so the house was filled with every gadget on the market and lots that were not.

The first morning a note came down with the orders for the day. They would all be out to lunch, but Master Roger would be in at about twelve. Would I cook the steak the butcher would be sending in.

I hadn't seen Master Roger, but at twelve o'clock I began to prepare the lunch for one in the dining room. Soon after twelve there was a ring at the door. It was my job in the morning to answer the door and the house parlour maid's in the afternoon. I opened the door. There stood a nice young man and a lovely friendly dog. I stood back for them to enter thinking that this was Master Roger, but the man patted the dog and said 'goodbye Roger', then raised his hat to me and went away. Master Roger was the dog.

When I told the other girl that I had cooked mushrooms and onions for the dog's dinner, we just stood and howled with laughter. No-one had thought to tell me about Roger. It never got called Master in the kitchen, but he was very friendly and couldn't help what his master did. I ask you – fancy calling a dog Master.

After a while I went back to Tenterden to stay nights with Auntie Bea as she had not been too well, so I got a daily job and was in with her in the night. I liked this. I could now have time to join things which I hadn't been able to before. I fancied doing country dancing, so I joined the Tenterden folk dance team. We met every Thursday and had a teacher to show us how to do the dance properly. We often went to other folk dance clubs, so I got about a bit and met new people. I was to meet the vicar's daughter once again and she still managed to bring out the worst in me. It happened like this. We were invited to the Canterbury folk dance party and were the guests of the vicar's daughter. At the hall she came along the room shaking hands with each one of us. Then she came to me. She put out her hand to shake mine then realised who I was. The look she gave me was one of amazement. I was the last person she had expected to see, especially there, but it wasn't long before she had recovered sufficiently to say how do you do and pass on. I often wished I could have met her as an equal or been able to have talked to her in a natural way and get that feeling out of my system. Actually she was a very good natured woman and I am sure she would have been horrified to know how she made me feel. I never did get the chance to break down the 'wrong feeling' between us and I am rather sorry. Perhaps if I could have made the effort to speak to her and say how she made me feel, things would have been different and I would not have the guilty feeling that it was my fault.

A job came up at the bank in Tenterden, so I took it on as a more permanent position. Here there was plenty to do, but the family was German, not that their nationality was anything against them, but it was a different way of living from what I had known previously. Everything was locked up, including the food. I was told that good housewives always locked up their store cupboards. This I could understand, but not the ordinary things like butter – this was doled out daily even to the dining room. They had to live on a budget. No wonder they are such good managers – they have had the life-long experience. The final crunch came when I found a £1.00 note carefully tucked under the stair carpet and the same day found another one on a ledge inside the wash basin. It was perched on the ledge that held up the basin, right over the used chamber pots which I was about to empty. That did it. I just pushed the note off the ledge and let it fall into the chamber, then took the pot with the note in it to the lady of the house. She was in the bathroom at the time and I told her what I had found in the pot. I had a right up-and-downer with her. I said I had brought good references with me and resented having notes left about for me to find. Once again she said that it was the place of every good housewife to test the honesty of her staff and not to rely on references of former employers. As to the note in the wash basin, that was to see if I had dusted the ledge or not. Then I saw red. I left there and then and forfeited the month's money in lieu. Her husband called later with the money for the time I had been there, and apologised for what had happened. His wife did not see things the way we did in England. That was very nice of him and I said so. He also said I could apply for a reference if I wished as they had no fault to find with my work.

I got work at another house on the same day and settled down quite happily with the owner and his daughter. Both were away quite a lot and were glad that I need not live in as they preferred to shut the house up leaving me to keep it dusted.

I stayed there until I married.

'Someone whistled after me' – Syd as a young man.

Chapter 14

MARRIAGE

Up until now I had not met or associated with boys, for there was always that dreadful fear of going the same way as my mother, and I tended to be ill at ease when talking with boys or men. Of course I had my secret crushes, but they were kept to myself. I was never able to talk or exchange confidences with other girls. After all I had been out of circulation when the girls I went to school with were going through their silly phases.

I had a secret crush on a boy for a long time, but he never knew, and I had no idea how to manage to meet him, so it died a natural death. Then for a period I went out on my time off with a nice boy, but that too petered out. For a while I corresponded with a boy in the navy. He was younger than me and this time it was he who had the crush on me, a case of an attraction to an older girl. I soon found him a bore, so I stopped writing to him.

One day when I was biking across the field home someone whistled after me. I turned round. It was the boy who had recently moved into a cottage on the farm near me. I tossed my head and went on, but I met him very often when I went to work and in the end stopped to chat with him. This was the start of the story which was to end with our wedding.

My future husband was the eldest of a family of seven. He earned 21/- each week of which he paid £1 to his mother. His father earned 30/- a week which, when he had paid out the rent and the insurance left about 25/- a week to bring up a family of six. Syd's money paid his keep and overtime bought all his clothes, so the 1/- pocket money, which was all he had, gave him nine pence for the pictures and three pence for sweets. All during the summer both father and son did do a bit of overtime and Syd also did a bit of gardening as well. Then, in the winter, there would be beating sometimes on a Saturday, when they would be paid so much and their dinner. It was this extra money, together with what I earned, that bought the furniture for our home.

I was working six days a week, and on Sundays went to a pub at Reading Street to help out there. I did the whole place out and occasionally got an extra job when the licensee had a party coming in for a meal. This was mostly in the summer. I worked like a Trojan that last year before we were married. We couldn't expect any help from Syd's parents as his mother was again expecting, and money was very tight. No-one today can realise what a struggle it was to bring up a family in those days. There was no family allowance, neither was there a free doctor for the children or the wife. The husband alone got free medicine and free doctor; for the rest it just meant that when there was a little outstanding debt, advice from the doctor was only sought as a last resort. No doubt that was why mortality was so much higher at that time. When a baby was

The Hatcher's wedding day, in September 1930.

to be born, then it was a case of save every penny or make do. My mother made nappies out of shirt tails. She would sew round all four sides, then run a stitch across from corner to corner both ways. There were no bales brought in, and no maternity grants. The husband did get some sort of insurance after it was over. I can't remember what it was but it didn't pay for the midwife. How Syd's mother managed I cannot think.

We were married at Tenterden in 1930. Syd's parents gave us the first week's wages as a wedding present. We felt we ought not take it, but they would have felt worse if they hadn't given anything at all, so we accepted it. We were married in September, the day before Syd finished hop drying. He didn't get home till eleven in the morning. We began to wonder whether he would make it. The hop dryer was very sorry, but the hops waited for no man, wedding or no wedding, so Syd had to stay until the pressing was done.

Auntie Bea's sister was very dear to me. She had promised that if I married respectably she would give me the wedding outfit. We found a lovely piece of silky material in an apricot colour. It was plain, no pattern, but it was not big enough, so we bought some more material in the same shade and took it along to the dressmaker we knew and she made a lovely job of it. I got a large floppy hat to go with it. It's a funny thing, I recently saw the identical dress in white in a shop in Maidstone, so the fashion had come in again, and so had the floppy hats.

My employer's daughter made the wedding cake and the farmer's wife I had gone to from the Union gave me a lovely tea service and her sister four towels. Actually the people I helped out on my off times all gave presents, so we really started off far better than Syd's mum and dad had. A friend I knew was going to live with her sister and wanted to sell her home, so once again we were lucky. We got beds, chairs, baths, tables, the lot, all at a low figure for the ready cash. I had received two pounds from a Sunday school teacher I had almost forgotten, which seemed a gold mine to me. Syd got his extra for being in the oast day and night, so we started off without any debts.

Our first cottage at Tenterden was really just two rooms, with a scullery leading off the kitchen, and a second bedroom having no fourth wall, only a banister rail, as it led from the side of the stairway and was really just a landing. We had a bucket privy outside, and a tap over the sink, but no outlook, as a very high wall was just outside our kitchen window and we had no other living room.

A year later, we moved to a cottage on the farm Syd worked on. It had been the old farmhouse but with conversion, was now three cottages. We had the first one; one large room with an old fireplace big enough to sit round each side without being in the main room. We had only wood for this which Syd was allowed to get and cut down. We lived surrounded by woods and fields, so heating was no problem. There was a huge pantry bigger than many living-rooms, and a scullery with a real copper tub. Upstairs was not so nice, one large room divided into two, with the dividing wall going through the middle of the fireplace. There were two attics, but one always got fleas if one went into them. No amount of scrubbing, Keatings, Jeyes Fluid, or any other insecticide could get rid of them, so we never used them. It was quite common to get an occasional flea in the country. I sometimes helped my mistress to search the blankets if they had been brought home from the fields but this attic was something different. The fleas just ran up one's legs, but they didn't come downstairs. Once again we had bucket privies, but we had to share with a neighbour, and we sometimes had trouble about emptying them.

Water came from a well outside the third cottage which was used by all three cottage dwellers as well as by two more families who lived three fields away. They had to come to the well for every bit of water they needed unless they had plenty of rain when they could catch some for washing purposes. We had to use candles and oil lamps for lighting but one became careful about using them, so there were not as many fires as one might have expected with naked flames and smoky lamps.

Later we moved to the third cottage. Now *we* had the well outside our cottage, but it had one drawback. The man who came to live in our old place had a large family and he would fill up the copper once each day for his wife to use from, but he *would* leave the lid up until he had finished, and often forgot to put it down at the end. Joyce, my daughter, might be playing outside, and I wouldn't hear him coming, so I was on tenterhooks always in case she was outside and fell down the well. Another thing I hated about that well was the fact that there was often a huge slug in it. The other people weren't concerned and said it would 'clear the water', but I hated it.

I kept my job for quite a while after we were married, so it gave us a chance to get a few more things for the home. Syd had a new brother by then and soon after that Syd's dad was stood off one winter. That was a dreadful time for us. There was no dole, only something called Parish relief. This was something that the vicar of the parish gave out to those in want, and this was one time when Syd's parents were in real need. I offered to go and see the vicar, though it was not the one I knew before, and in fact he had not been there very long. I was ushered into the drawing room by the parlour maid. Presently, the vicar came in to see what it was I wanted. I started to say that I was there for my mother-in-law, when the vicar stopped me. 'Why are you here instead of her?' he said. I tried to explain that there was a large family and as I had a bike and the cottage was a long way off I had come instead. Then we went through a whole list of questions, why did the children not come to Sunday school – I explained that it needed all the weekend to get the school clothes washed and ready for school on Monday. Nobody can imagine today what a job it was to keep children clothed decently on a farm worker's wage. No-one had best clothes, not if they were farm workers, unless they had relatives who were better off than themselves.

Finally, the vicar gave me a chit to take to the grocer for ten shillings' worth of goods, but I was to present the list to him first, so that he could satisfy himself that we were not buying unnecessary items. When I took the list back, the jar of paste was struck off, so we put on rice instead, it being about the same price. It was the first and only time we went for parish relief. No doubt it was meant to make us feel like beggars, otherwise they would have had all sorts of people begging at the vicar's door. The next week we found all the small potatoes and gave them to Syd's mother, and with a jar or two of jam and three pennyworth of bones, plus a bag of flour, somehow they got through. Rather than go and ask for help again for them, I would keep them myself, but we didn't have to; the farmer had him back the next week and shortly afterwards he got another job and moved away. Syd's parents were a lot better off there at the new job. There was work for the wife on the fruit and hop farm, so life was easier for them. I missed them quite a bit for I was very fond of my mother-in-law. All the old talk about mothers-in-law was not right in my case.

My first baby was born in June of the following year. Now I found out at first hand how hard it was to manage to get all I needed for the baby on our wage. We were lucky, for I did have a maternity grant for the first child as I worked up till a few days before my little girl was born. In fact I was still working the night previously because the lady I was employed by was opening a shop on the following day, and I had been doing it out. I had intended to go in first thing in the morning to give a final polish to everything, but in the night my daughter decided to arrive three weeks early, so I had to send a message by Syd to say I would not be there. Joyce arrived at four in the afternoon, a lovely little seven pound baby. I was now a mother, and another phase of life began.

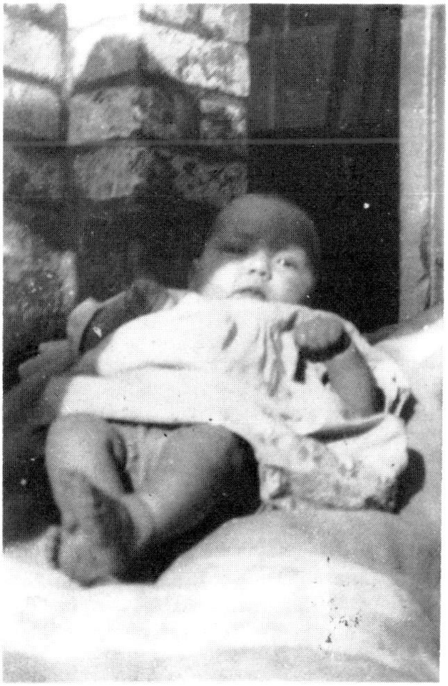

Baby Joyce, aged 3½ months.

Somehow I managed to do some sort of work to help out the family budget. In the summer there was work in the fruit fields, and in the winter I did a Saturday cleaning job at a shop. This did bring me in a little money to spend on clothes. Usually I had a doctor's bill to pay with the hop-tying money, just as my mother-in-law had done in the past. Later when Joyce was old enough to go to school, there was a variety of work which was not available for people with small children. Now I could do strawberry picking. No-one with a small child would be employed for this work, for the children would get on the beds and trample on the fruit, or so said the employers. Strawberry picking was nothing like it is today. We began in the early hours of the morning, about four o'clock as a rule. At ten, work stopped until about four in the afternoon, then we carried on till nine. We would be almost lying down in the rows by then, but the season only lasted a few weeks so we got what we could when we could.

Rain stopped work for a few hours, so sometimes we would be there on the farm waiting nearly all day and perhaps not getting any work in at all, when all the time we could have been at home doing our own work, but that was the hazard of fruit picking. Plum picking was quite a different matter. These were picked piecework, so the faster we worked, the more money we earned. When I started work on the land, daywork was paid 5½d an hour, but in piecework one could earn something like 15/- a week. Syd's weekly wage was one pound fifteen shillings by the time the second world war broke out.

A rare outing. Auntie Bea, with Dorothy's mother carrying Jo.

Chapter 15

THE WAR YEARS

The war made a great difference to us. In 1939, eight years after Joyce was born, I had another little girl, but now women could get a job on a farm anywhere, with or without children. After all, the men were in the army unless they were wanted for growing food, which was the case for some farm workers. All conscientious objectors were sent to help and some of them must have found it very hard going, but it was their choice. In the case of a farm worker, they didn't get a choice. They had to stay and help grow the country's food.

All that first year Syd was working from daylight till dark, during the summertime that is. I went to help out on the small farm of a friend where strawberries and a bit of wheat were grown. I slept in so as to be there first thing in the morning. My little girl Judy came with me, while Joyce stayed with Auntie Bea. Syd came to work all day Sunday, so we really were taking in the money. Actually it was this which made such a difference to the average working man: wages rose and rose as the need to grow food became important. Later I went to work on a larger farm where there was a bigger variety of crops. Blackcurrants were needed by the Government as they contained so much vitamin C. We were not allowed to buy them, only from private peoples' gardens. There were also peas, plums and apples to be picked, as well as hoeing, haymaking, harvesting and threshing. I worked all the year round, then and in the years to follow.

How the pattern of farm work had altered. No longer did we see women in their sun bonnets turning the hay in the fields. Instead we wore our tin hats around our waists, for since they had been issued they went everywhere with us. For me that was quite a problem as I had to bike to town taking my gas mask (and in holiday time the two girls' gas masks) as well as my tin helmet. One woman on the farm would wear hers loosely around her waist, so that when she bent over, as most of our work entailed doing, the hat sat loosely on her bottom. It wasn't any good telling her what it looked like. She would just wear it that way, to the glee of all passing people. I can't blame them, she really did look funny.

For the first time since we were married, we saved a bit of money in the bank. Although we saved thirty pounds during those war years, there wasn't anything to buy. Things like combs, hairpins and grips became unobtainable. Clothes were scarce. It was quite the thing to go bare legged and bare headed. The church allowed one to go in without a hat on, although most people put on a handkerchief.

The horror of war was all round us now. We had radio to give us the news, which we had not had in the previous war. Also the London people came down to do the fruit picking, those who were not in munitions that is. Then one hop picking year, the year of the Battle of Britain, they came down as usual, but on

A haystack in the making.

Harvesting near Cranbrook.

the second night the bombers came over all night, wave after wave of them, and we had no shelters. This was followed by a day of overhead fights with our first line of defence over their heads. That was enough, they all packed up and went home, and who can blame them. They had shelters at home; here there was nothing.

The war was different from the peaceful life of the country. The noise of the bombers assembling overhead each day for their various missions, the continuous dog fights, the challenge of making a meal out of half a pie or reconstituted egg, and jam from carrots and a jelly, all kept us on our toes.

I may have found it easier than some, for all my married life I had been used to being careful, to plan so that a meal of some sort was served each day. We did keep chickens, and in the country they could roam free and get all their own food, with scraps from our table and potato peelings boiled and mixed with oats for a mash. The children had bantams too and a couple of guinea fowl. The noise they made before going to roost had to be heard to be believed. They would walk suspiciously round the chicken house until all the other hens were inside, then with a loud squawking noise they would race round and round the hut. Suddenly one made a dash for the doorway, and the other followed. They followed this pattern all the time we had them. They do lay a very rich egg, quite big for their size.

If a hen went off laying and we thought it wouldn't be laying many more times, then we had an occasional so-called chicken. It was usually done in a casserole. Apart from that we had the same as the others except for harvest rations, and the extra allowance of cheese for agricultural workers. During the winter we were allowed to ferret for rabbits, so I mostly had at least one a week during the winter months. We did get by fairly well, but I used to long for the end of rationing. There was so much one could not get, like shoelaces, even string. We saved money because we hadn't anything to spend it on. Christmas was hard, because the only things we could buy were goods not up to standard for export, such as Judy's Christopher, a doll with a squashed-in face.

From the farm at Tenterden we moved to Benenden, to another very old house, now demolished. There was still no electricity or gas, but we had a tap at the top of the garden, one step nearer to civilization. There were steps at the back leading to a spring, so I imagine the tap had been a fairly recent improvement. There were bees in the wall here, and a baker's oven which I only used to store cleaning materials, and a nice road running alongside the cottage to the main road. But I never liked living at Benenden, and I can't think why. Syd didn't like the work. He was used to tractor and hop work, ploughing and so on. Here he was milking and calf rearing, so once again off we went back to Tenterden.

The bungalow we went to was an old army pre-fab, with all-wood floors – much warmer than the previous cottage. It had a flush lavatory, tap over the sink, and a kitchen range. It was near the main road, but had no electricity. I liked it, even though it was just at the back of the old Union in Tenterden, of which I have many unhappy memories. It was here in 1943 that Gerald was born at

The bungalow by the Union.

twenty past one, double summer time, so by the clock he was born on March 10th and by the sun, March 9th. He arrived in the midst of a nasty raid and the midwife had to come through barricades to get to me. There were parachutists down somewhere so barriers were up on all the roads and she was told to stay with me until morning.

The planes seemed to be concentrating on Hastings way but a lot came through to us and were intercepted overhead by the fighters. To add to our troubles my Tilley lamp went out, then the fire. I had an anthracite stove in the bedroom, and the wind must have changed, for it suddenly started blowing out fumes into the room. I had to get up with Gerald, only a few hours old, and sit by the kitchen fire until it cleared – that was a night. Our midwife was a wonderful woman. For years she had gone out in all weathers on her bike to deliver

Judy and Gerald.

babies and give advice to new mums. She came down to me at the old cottage with both her knees out of her stockings, having fallen down on our very rutty lane on her bike. I told her I wouldn't need her any more, now she had brought my son. 'There's gratitude for you' she said, 'I bring what you ordered and you straight away give me the sack.' Mothers always stayed in bed for the full nine days after a birth and on the tenth day I got up. On the twelfth day, the nurse came and I had already bathed the baby. All she came for was just to see that everything was all right.

One day, I heard a siren on the coast go, and it must have been a little sneak raid for it was nine o'clock in the morning. A plane would come in, cut out its engines, then bomb whatever it had come over for. I wrapped Gerald up and got under the kitchen table with Judith, who had just been given a horse and cart by one of the German prisoners. They were always making things like that, men walking up ladders, chickens pecking corn off a little stand. They were a handy race of people who could make anything out of anything. They were not supposed to, and we were not supposed to take anything or give anything either, but they had children back in their homes and if it gave them pleasure to give something to my little girl, no doubt they could feel it was the next best thing to making something for their own children. We would slip them the odd cigarette or piece of cake; after all Syd worked with them all day. Anyway, on this day Judy suddenly darted out from under the table to bring in her horse and cart to safety.

Night raids were on, with quite a different pattern to day ones. Search lights would fix onto a plane and suddenly all around would pinpoint it. Sometimes it kept coming on with one search light going out of range and another taking over, 'guiding them in' we used to say, but of course the guns were firing at them all the time. Then there would be a sudden flare and the plane was gone. Sometimes the search lights on one particular plane would all go out and then one of our planes would take over. Many still got through of course to the next raid. Night raids were beautiful to watch – if only it had not been for such a dreadful reason. It was like a gigantic firework display. By now we had 'flaming onions'. These were streams of shells fired at the enemy and every other one seemed to be alight until suddenly it was like a string of flaming lights, leaving the ground and getting closer and closer to the target. What with that and the flashing coastal guns and the tracer bullets in the sky and the search lights everywhere, there was plenty to watch in the night sky.

One dreadful night when we had been in the thick of the bombing, it was thought that an unexploded bomb was nearby. It turned out later that no bomb was found, but when we went back, our house had been vandalised. Things were all over the place. A lot of photos were missing including one of Ellen Terry which was signed, and one of my little girl taken on her first birthday just as she was taking her first step.

Then we had a new terror. One evening there was a noise overhead like somebody riding a motor bike over our roof. We rushed outside. It looked like a small plane with a flame coming out of its tail. We thought at first it was a small plane which had been hit, but then came another and another and we realised Hitler's promised 'secret weapon' had arrived, the doodle bug. Some called it the buzz bomb. Whatever it was called, the thing was nasty. It would go on a course for London and then its engine would cut out and it would fall to the ground, exploding on impact. The noise it made was dreadful, but we soon got used to it, and at least once it had gone over we were safe. There were three routes. Syd and I worked out that if it came in on either side of the trees it missed us, but if it came straight over the top, then it would come over us too. Lots of engines cut out long before getting to London. In fact many cut out over the sea. There was always the danger of one coming down overhead.

The American pilots would hang about coming back from their particular mission hoping to intercept one of them. They would fly alongside hoping to tip the wings. They weren't always successful and they could put them onto a different course. It was a very dangerous thing to do as one Polish pilot found to his cost. He had fired into the tail of the thing as he flew behind it, but it blew up straight away and the pilot flew straight into the blast and we saw bits of the plane spiralling down to the ground. He came down near Benenden where we were picking peas on a farm nearby at the time.

My sister-in-law and I had two very nasty experiences, one while we were working there. A buzz bomb engine cut out just above the currant field where we were picking. I grabbed Gerald and lay on him waiting for the explosion. I doubt if it would have saved him, but one has to do something. It exploded in the wood at the bottom of the field and most of the blast went over our heads. We were very near to it and my face was numb for the rest of the day. The smoke of the explosion was all around us. I think those higher up in the field and further away from us got the full blast, more than we did. There was one thing I never lived down over that. When I got up and picked Gerald up it appeared that I had laid him on a thistle. He wasn't worried about the doodle bug, oh dear no. He was far more upset that I hadn't looked where I had put him.

Another time we were waiting for the bus to take us back to Tenterden. Just as it stopped and we were getting on, a doodle bug came over. 'Everyone out' shouted the conductor and we all got off and lay alongside the bus until it had gone over. Now there was a gun unit in the field over the hedge and they opened fire at it, so we were in the thick smoke again. If it had been brought down it might have come right on us, so we were thankful that it went over unharmed. There were gun units in fields all over the countryside. We got on with our jobs and they got on with theirs.

Our defence people soon got the measure of those buzz bombs. Barrage balloons were put up all over London and they could be set at a height so that they would be in the flight path of the bombs. Many were brought down by the cables of the barrage balloons. As weapons they were not really accurate and our folks soon discovered the sites of the launching pads and bombed them out of existence.

Then came a new menace. The doodle bug was the V1 but the V2 was a rocket. The explosion came first and then the sound it made going overhead came afterwards. This was nasty. There just wasn't anything anyone could do except carry on as usual. After all, one hit by one of those things and it would all be over and one wouldn't know anything about it.

We had been issued with indoor shelters by now, so we could stay in bed and try to forget everything. There was nothing we could do. We made a bed for Gerald along the top of our pillows. The two girls had been evacuated. Joyce was getting nervy and the chance came for them to go to Dulverton in Somerset. Their school teacher went with them and they were very fortunate to be selected by the lady who was in charge of the evacuation in that area. The place they stayed at was a nice house, near the river. The old nanny had come back to stay for the duration and took over the care of my two. Judy lapped it all up, but Joyce was not quite so happy about it. There was a pony and a nursery play room, complete with rocking horse. I thought they were very fortunate and I was glad they were together. I could have gone with Gerald, but I wouldn't leave Syd. He was working all hours, it being double summer time, for it was light until eleven each evening. We arranged for Auntie Bea to have a shelter too, and she had it until she died, in that shelter, on Judy's sixth birthday.

Our neighbours in the harvest field.

Life did have a happier side to it though, and there was always something to laugh at. One good thing came out of it – 'class distinction' went by the board. Petrol was rationed, or should I say unobtainable to all except doctors, and people using it for the country. Since everyone used the buses more, all the separate seats were taken out and a seat put in running all round the bus, leaving a big empty space in the middle. We soon dubbed it the 'cattle truck', but it was possible to get lots more people in the bus. First come had the seats, and the rest squashed in. One couldn't fall over as there were too many bodies: we held each other up. So people who wouldn't have thought of talking in the ordinary way just chatted amongst themselves, about the raids, the weather and the rationing. We were a friendly lot during the war days and for a long time after. In fact things have never gone back to that stage again.

We had two other kinds of warfare, the leaflet raids and Lord Haw Haw, the man turned traitor. The leaflets telling their side of the story were brought over and dropped by planes. It was all very laughable, and didn't upset us at all. In fact we just had a good laugh and the kids gathered up as many as they could for a paper chase. It hurt them more than it hurt us as they had the expense of it. Lord Haw Haw was a different matter altogether. He had a wavelength of his own and just poured out propaganda. That wasn't too bad, as we were not that gullible, but then he came in between the news items as the nine o'clock news was broadcast. The ghastly chuckle started and our newsreader would read a line of news, then Lord Haw Haw would put in a line of his own. It just gave us a lot more light relief. Soon he was cut out.

Rationing was in force throughout the war and for sometime afterwards. We got something like 2 ounces of cheese, butter, margarine or other fat. We had an agriculture allowance as well, so we were well away. I had more cheese than I needed because there were two of us working on the farm, but I managed to swap some for sugar with someone who kept bees, as they were allowed a little extra sugar. Once a month we used up our points and these could be spent on a variety of items such as syrup, jam, cereal, tins of meat, fish etc. At one time meat ration was six pennyworth of fresh meat and two pennyworth of corned beef per week, per person. Offal was free, but difficult to get. I gave up three books of egg ration for chicken feed, but I kept the other two books, so I had one or two eggs when my chickens stopped laying. We would all boil up potato peel to mix with the meal to help them out. We also got harvest ration during the summer months for doing the harvesting and such like, so foodwise we were well enough. We could get agricultural pies from the baker and heated up with plenty of vegetables and gravy, it was possible to make a meal with these. Sweets also were on ration, one book a week divided amongst all five of us and the last book lodged with the confectioner for special occasions. America sent over a consignment of 'lease lend' foods. One was a lovely tin of sausage meat. It was really good and had enough fat around it to make twenty-four tiny sausage rolls for a party, such as Christmas or a birthday. Recipes for sugarless foods were in all the books. One was for carrot jam; boil the carrots, mash them, add the liquor to an orange jelly and then add the mashed carrot and pot it. Well, it got eaten anyway. We had reconstituted eggs and they were all right for baking, but you can't put a spoonful of egg mixture in for a boiled egg, can you. Working on a fruit farm we got a lot of 'specked' fruit, at least apples.

The war finally came to an end, but rationing lasted a long time after, but who cared. We could walk about in safety once more and sleep without any worries. Our two little girls came back. Judy had grown a lot and looked really bonny. Joyce wasn't so well-looking, so perhaps it was her age and not the bombing that had upset her. We were glad to have them back and for them to see their little brother and how he had grown.

One sad thing I witnessed. Auntie Bea had a friend, a poor woman who had married late in life and had only one son. He had been through the war and was missing, believed killed. Later she learned that he was in a prisoner-of-war camp. Then, at the end of the war, the prisoners were released from the camp, but the journey was too much for him and he had died in hospital just before he could reach his own home again. That poor woman sat just staring into space. All the chocolates and things she had saved out of her ration for when Harry came home were all there in her cupboard. I had never seen such a look on anyone's face before, and I hope I never do again. Within two months she was dead, life had nothing more for her. There must have been many such stories that could have been told after the war, but that was the one I knew of.

A birthday trip to Hastings.

The end of the war came in two stages, Victory in Europe and Victory in Japan, so we had two lots of celebrations. VE day was a gathering almost impromptu. We heard by word of mouth that everyone who wished could meet out in the road in the evening, outside the town hall, so we wrapped up Gerald in his pram and set off. It was a lovely get-together to rejoice, everyone meeting on an equal footing. Music came from a loudspeaker from inside the town hall. There were no street parties, no free food, no drinks – we didn't need them. All we wanted was to get together to rejoice and to dance about, just to be there all together. Then we went back home to rationing, to work, to everyday happenings, but in safety. The celebrations for VJ day were very different. A special day was arranged for rejoicing and getting together in the recreation field, but somehow there wasn't the same spontaneous enthusiasm that we had experienced outside the town hall on VE day. Our fruit farmer laid on an outing to Brighton, which we enjoyed. We could go to the seaside again as the beaches were no longer cordoned off. I had not been to Hastings during the whole of the war, for we couldn't afford many outings like that at that time.

But we did celebrate Joyce's 14th birthday with a trip to the seaside. Syd met us at the bus-stop, having managed to get the day off, and Joyce had to guess where we were going.

Chapter 16

A POST-WAR INTERLUDE IN LEICESTERSHIRE

The war was over, but things would never be the same again. We in the country, especially around Tenterden, had had our full share of the dogfights and stray sticks of bombs. When fighters overhead attacked bombers on their way in to London, they promptly dropped their load and got out as soon as they could, if they were lucky.

However very little damage had been done to property, the worst case I knew of being a cottage on the Sanatorium estate, and that was hit by a Doodle Bug which came in very low, first over our bungalow, and then in a direct line to the cottage, running straight into it. Another incident involved a house on the Benenden to Cranbrook road which had been occupied by soldiers who had left that morning. A new contingent was to take it over the same evening, but it was bombed during the day. Two people were killed at a bungalow at Beech House by a rocket. The rebuilding did not alter the look of the countryside much, and any really old house was rebuilt much as it had been before. It seemed years before the authorities got round to filling up all the bomb craters, and there were plenty of those around.

The last of the soldiers came home, those who had had to stay to put things straight, or whatever the mopping-up operation after a war entails. Rationing lasted for a long time. I believe that sweets were the last to come off, but even when they did they were scarce, so in fact they were still rationed, as retailers made sure their regulars got their usual supply before serving all and sundry.

My children were growing up. Joyce, my eldest, had left school and was starting as an apprentice to learn shorthand and typing. I was determined to give my children the best start we could, so she would go to the office, help generally until the students came in, then she would take her place and study along with the paying ones.

To pay for this I went out early mornings cleaning, 7 till 8.30, and this paid the part fee which was what I had to pay for the tuition. Jo brought Gerald up to the office door and I met her there, leaving my bike for Jo to bring home, and I would wheel Gerald home or around the shops. He had called his sister Jo as he couldn't say Joyce, so she has been Jo to this day.

Gerald had been having middle ear trouble, and later on when the soldiers from the Belsen camps or P.O.W. camps came over and were put in what is now Homewood School, a wave of dysentery broke out among young babies or very old people. It was a trying period for all mothers.

Gerald, being below par because of his middle ear trouble, went down with the dysentery, and for a time he was very ill. The doctor prescribed grated raw apple. It seemed a ridiculous thing to give him, and so the doctor said, but he

The Church at Foston, from a 1792 print.

told me to trust him, and so I did. The worst of the complaint began to clear up, but he was still very ill.

The effects of that illness lasted for three years, and his mouth would occasionally break out with infection. We could soon clear it up with a violet mixture, but I was glad when he grew out of that. Impetigo was always associated with dirt and dirty people.

He grew out of the impetigo and the dysentery, but the middle ear trouble continued until he was seven. This meant I couldn't continue for a spell with all the work I had been doing, but I did an early hour job and got paid quite well for it.

We moved away from Tenterden about this time. Syd's brother knew someone in Leicester who could get a farm job for both of them. We had a cottage at Foston, a hamlet with about eight cottages, one farm house, a Rectory and a Church. It must at sometime have been a lot bigger, for the gravestones in the Churchyard dated back to the Plague and the Great Fire of London. Some seemed to have come there and died. Foston was a mile from the village of Countesthorpe, four and a half miles from Leicester city centre, so we used to bike into town, at least I did, and got much shopping for my sister-in-law and myself. I'd never seen a queue before and here there were queues for everything, including oranges and bananas which were just coming back on the market. I waited for ages to get some in Leicester, but found that we'd already had our quota back in Tenterden, so that was a waste of time. I would queue for a long time for ½lb tomatoes. I needed two ½lbs, but I would have to queue all over again for some for my sister-in-law. I could have another lot if I bought a peach at 8d, which was dear for that time, but that is what I did. Often I would be nearly up to my turn and the seller would shout 'Closing for ½ hour's lunch', and there we would be. It would be quicker to wait for his return than to go to another stall. Shopping took all day as I had Gerald with me. He was always diving under the stall for dropped fruit or bad fruit, and I was afraid of him getting dysentery again. I got my tomatoes in the end, bought a peach and got my further ½lb for my sister-in-law, then gave the peach to Gerald. I knew that one was clean. He took one bite and handed it back to me and said 'Take its frock off, Mum'. He thought the downy skin was some sort of cover.

Jo got a job in a huge factory in the clerical department as an apprentice, and it was arranged that she would go to college when the new term started. The firm was called the British United Shoe Manufacturing Co., and had a staff of 4,000, so it was said great crowds came out when the siren went. Jo loved it, she had a chance to get on the typewriter addressing envelopes sometimes, but it was mostly just jobs like filing, but she had her foot on the first rung of the ladder or so we thought.

Judy started at the Leicester School and came home horrified, 'Mum' she said, 'The teacher called out six names and they all had to go and stand out in front of the class. The teacher said these children have lice in their hair, no-one must play with them,' and it appeared they were then sat in desks of their own.

Poor Judy couldn't have been more upset if she had been one of the unfortunates.

We all hated Leicester. What on earth made us go we now can't imagine. Things were scarce, and we were not known, so we had to keep going to the same shop to be known before we could get the odd food off ration, like offal.

We did have a nice cottage in a row of four, and had electric light and a Triplex stove, a sort of open fire but with two ovens at the side and a back boiler, so we had hot water, a hot and a cool oven and a fire to look at. It had no bathroom, but never having had one we never missed it and had a weekly tub in front of the fire with the kitchen door locked, as neighbours were very neighbourly there and just walked in uninvited. We had a sitting room there, our first. Up till then it had always been kitchen and scullery. The man in the end cottage was an electrician, but had left factory work to go on the farm as he didn't want to be called up. He was pretty clever, and made an electric ring out of two sandwich tins.

But . . . There was a very big 'but'! The toilets were in a row up the gardens, bucket affairs emptied by the Council every Monday. Gerald *would* go out to watch the lavy men, as he called them, and the smell was atrocious and reached all over the house.

'I missed the primroses'.

There is a tale that the woman who lived in the cottage before me actually sat on the toilet, and being deaf did not hear the lorry coming to empty the bucket. The first thing she knew was that the back of the privy opened and a hand removed the bucket. Anyway that's the tale and it could quite easily be true.

Now if I had hated Benenden, I loathed Leicester. No sooner did I put my foot on the ground than I wanted to go back. Syd didn't settle either. The work was plentiful, money was a little higher than in Kent, or it was on our farm, and their was plenty of overtime, but I missed the primroses, the woods and my own friends. The water was very hard, and scum came on washing so it needed a softening agent.

Jo loved her job though, but Syd decided to try and get back to the South, so on Bank Holiday Monday he had his weekend off (one in three weeks), and he and his brother were off on the train to Cranbrook where their mother was living.

That Saturday after they had gone a woman came to the door selling lucky heather, I bought some and she said if I crossed her hand with silver she would tell me my fortune. I had 6d which I gave her. 'You are not happy here' she said, 'and you will soon be going back near where you came from.' Now there was no way she could have known we were after a move, we didn't tell a soul as it wouldn't do to let the employer know before we were certain. I don't usually believe in gypsies' forecastings, but I felt in my bones that this was going to be one time when it would come true. I was waiting at the door when I heard Syd coming along the path. 'When do we go?' I asked. He thought I must have seen his brother beforehand and found out, but the fact remained the gypsy's prophecy came true, for within a fortnight we had left. We got a farm lorry which cost the two families £12. It had cost a lot more on the journey up, but the employer paid that. He was very good about our leaving, and said perhaps we might meet again, but I don't suppose we ever will.

My sister-in-law and I went ahead with the children. The two men and our dog Trixie came with the lorry. Poor Jo, she was so upset, she had settled down at the office, her future would be secure and now we were uprooting her from all she liked, so she sulked in the train all the way home. It wasn't until we were nearly home (Syd's Mum's) that she perked up and became more agreeable. We spent the night at my mother-in-law's, then off to see Syd's new employer and get the key. There was no cottage for my sister-in-law, but we offered to house her furniture until they could get one.

After a month or two the converted oast house became vacant, and both families moved in, but later Syd's brother got a job at his old employer's and went back there to live.

Chapter 17

SISSINGHURST

The oasthouse was on the Golford-Benenden road at the end of the Sissinghurst boundary. Here we had big square rooms, a large garden, an apple tree, orchards all round and woods to play in. Although there was no electricity, so that it was back to Tilley lamps and candles for us, water was laid on and we had a boiler for heating it. We had nice roomy bedrooms and a lovely bathroom, with a wonderful view at blossom time. As the house was on a hill we could see a long way around.

My kitchen was big and we had a huge meal table in the middle, and one wall covered with lino to take the darts which missed the dartboard. There were an awful lot of steps up to the back door and down into the kitchen, but my family loved that house. The only snag was that we had so many windows and I hated window-cleaning. There were four in the kitchen, and two glass doors, and a window and three glass doors in the inner hall. Outside the kitchen window was a huge water tank, and it wasn't long before it was stocked up with goldfish and tiddlers and other things fished with a jam jar from ponds and ditches.

Jo got a job on the farm with two other girls and took to farm work like a duck takes to water. One of the other girls was later to become her sister-in-law.

I had my mother to live with me now. I had tried unsuccessfully quite a few times, but then out of the blue I had a letter to say that relatives were now being encouraged to take their mothers or other dependants into their homes. A pension or social security would be provided. I had been having Mother out for visits weekends for quite a while and had bought her a dress, shoes, hat and coat to come out in, for the clothes that she was usually dressed in were very old.

When I arrived to take her out for the last time I was absolutely staggered to see how little she had, after 38 years of being shut away from the world. The only clothes she had were what she stood up in and that was a miscellaneous collection of cast offs. There wasn't even a nightdress for her to go to bed in that night, and no change of clothes. Her vest was a man's, the half-sleeve button through type. Surely they could have sent her out respectably dressed after all those years. I had to rig her out with two changes of clothes right through, and a decent pair of shoes.

Poor Mother. When she came out she was in the seventh heaven. After years of turning down my application, finally the powers that be seemed only too pleased to get rid of her.

It took a lot of settling in though. In fact she was never really quite at ease with me. It was impossible to relax. She got on well with the children, and when I wasn't present would chatter to them as an equal, but as soon as I appeared she was a different person and seemed to treat me much as one of the attendants at

The converted oasthouse at Farningham.

the Union – I was in her mind 'over her'. Yet she was so willing to do anything I asked. We worked out a few duties which could be hers if she wished, so she did the table laying, wiping up the dishes and kept the fire made up if we had the stove on. It was nice to come home at lunch time to a hot meal on colder days, as she would put the potatoes on. I would prepare perhaps a casserole and a second course of some sort before I went, and Mother could attend to it, she was always so willing. One day I will never live down. I was working at the other end of the farm, and Syd's work was nearby, so he was home and waiting for his meal when I panted in. Gerald was home, as it was half term. We all ate our first course except Syd who had been reading the paper. I changed plates, and started putting the afters round; apple, then spoonfuls of custard, and reached Syd just as he started his casserole. Oops – before I could stop myself I had put a dollop of custard on his casserole. He just looked at his plate and said 'I've never had it with custard before.' That taught him to get on with his dinner!

Breakfast and midday meals were always a rush during the week, but we made up for it with a leisurely weekend.

Early morning was worst, Gerald always had something that wanted doing at the last minute. A strap would break, or he couldn't find something. One day he needed a last minute press to his trousers. I hurriedly got them done when he came rushing down, 'Mum, you've put the creases in the side instead of the front.' Back I took them and put in the proper creases. I was just going out the back door when I heard, 'Mum, I've got square trousers'. I hadn't taken out the side

Dorothy's brother George with their mother.

creases. I hurried off down the path before he could get me at it again. Life was never dull, and my lot say there will be plenty to remember me by when I'm gone.

Sunday morning was the highlight of the week. We would sit around the kitchen table, after breakfast, discussing the happenings of the week, the film Joyce had seen, what had happened at school and at work. There was no special timetable on Sunday, although the two youngsters did go to Sunday school.

We bought ornaments and pictures for Mother's room, and various things like new curtains and a pretty rug, but we could never make her look after her room herself, and she hoarded everything she picked up, any rubbish, a broken button or hinge, tin lids, match boxes, something we had thrown out. We had no electricity until later, so we took a candle up for her to go to bed, and we blew it out and left her with a nightlight and a torch. We had to turn her room out every so often because of all the rubbish she kept.

Another thing she did was to stand at the bottom of the garden looking over the hedge, just as she used to in the Union grounds. Yet she was free to go out whenever she liked, and she did every day, and talked quite freely to everyone. I was the one that she was uneasy with, yet when I used to have her out for a weekend before, she was quite at home with me. I don't really think I was the right person to look after her, but she was welcome to a home, she was after all my mother.

I did have a guilty feeling because I could never feel for her in the same way as I had for Auntie Bea when she had been alive, but I hadn't shown it, at least I don't think I did.

Mother stayed with us until a year before she died. By then she was quite senile and had to go away.

Joyce started going about with a boy living nearby and was married at eighteen. Her future mother-in-law had been evacuated from London and settled down on a farm, and her daughter worked with Joyce and they became friends and finally sisters-in-law. We all went to London to get the wedding outfits: I loved my day in the city.

It was the first time in my life that the money from the hop picking and Syd's hop drying was spent on clothes. There was so much that was needed. Joyce chose her dress and accessories and then it was my turn. I just couldn't make up my mind between a very pretty dress with beaded panel and coat, or a costume. Finally I did get the dress, but bought a very serviceable coat and hat to wear over it. After all I could show off the dress at the reception.

Joyce was very lucky as they had a cottage across at Cranbrook to go to after the wedding, which was at Sissinghurst church. It was a very cold typical November day. I got Judy ready in her blue bridesmaid's dress. The little girl next door was the other attendant, and I got myself ready and then of course something had to go wrong. I pressed Syd's new trousers. The jacket was very nice but the trousers looked as if they could do with a press, so I hastily did this and put them on Joyce's bed as she was changing in our room which was bigger, and then it happened – those trousers disappeared. We looked under the bed and in the drawers. They just weren't there. I hastily raked all our things out of the airing cupboard and all the drawers. They just weren't there. So, in desperation I pressed his second best trousers, the same navy luckily and he wore his new navy coat and his old navy trousers. I had to leave them then, no time to see if they looked all right. Perhaps it was as well that it was a misty day. No-one seemed to see that he had odd trousers on and the solemnity of the marriage service soon put it from my mind. The next day the trousers were discovered between the bed and the floor. I had looked under the bed but I hadn't thought to pull the bed away from the wall. Well, no wedding can go without a hitch, it seems. Joyce made a radiant bride, the first of my brood to leave the nest. Times were still not easy and Joyce was very young to take on the running of a home and later a family.

Soon after we moved to the oasthouse Gerald became very ill, suddenly. We sent for the doctor who came out before surgery. He said he would call again the next day, but if I was anxious I was not to hesitate but to call him. Gerald appeared to sleep in the afternoon so I thought 'that's good, he will be better when he wakes up'. It had often happened with my children, they would go to bed really poorly, then have a sound sleep and awake refreshed. At five o'clock the doctor returned, and he looked very grave. He said he must get him into hospital at once. He wasn't sleeping but in a coma. That was a never-to-be-forgotten night. I went up with the ambulance while Syd stayed to give Judy her meal. I was told I must stay at the hospital, and later in the evening Syd arrived: a friendly bus driver had diverted his bus all the way up to the hospital at Tunbridge Wells. He had been sent for. They found us a bed but we couldn't sleep. We were not allowed to see Gerald, parents didn't in those days. The authorities thought it unsettled the child to see his friends or his parents, so I never saw him again until I went to fetch him home, some months later.

He had cerebral meningitis and was in a critical condition. It was gratifying to be told by the sister that had he not been in top condition he would have died. A year later we went to the hospital and with the removal of tonsils and adenoids he never looked back.

No child could have had a better playground than my two youngest. Judy was a great tomboy, and was never happier than when climbing trees and doing handstands etc.

On one occasion I called the children into tea, but could get no answer. I was always told which way and where they were going. This had been a rule, for with their love of tree climbing anything could have happened (but never did). We felt they should use their leisure time as they liked, provided they didn't get into any mischief, but say where they were going and show us any new contraptions. On going down to find them, I could hear music from under my feet. I was standing just inside the wood by a steep bank. Those two had scooped out a hole in the side of the bank big enough for both to get in, and had our wireless in there as well. That had to be banned, they could have been buried alive and no-one would have known where they were. It's a wonder the bank didn't cave in as I stood on it. Another prank – Gerald seemed to be the one – he had lashed together two drums, empty, and told me to come and see their boat. As I neared the spot they ran ahead and I arrived to my horror, to see them sitting astride these drums paddling across the filthiest pond that was on the farm. Their legs! Fortunately they had put on wellies, but they were stirring up the thick black sludge from the bottom. They could have caught a fever. Thank goodness they got me to see their invention.

Later Gerald made a rope ladder out of old hop string, and a good job he had made of it. He had it fixed across a steep bank at the top of the trees. He also made a clever lift by having an apple box on one rope and a seat on the other, arranged so that when he had climbed the ladder and the tree, he could sit in the seat and the box would come down. I shudder to think what had happened while he perfected that, since the drop down that slope was enormous.

Dorothy hop-picking with her sister-in-law at Stream Farm.

Chapter 18

VILLAGE LIFE

I had plenty of work hop training, hoeing, apple picking, grading and so on. Hop picking was my favourite job, and nothing can ever replace the old way of picking hops. At seven in the morning one could go across fields and through the woods to the hop garden, dew would be on everything, millions of cobwebs on the hedges and trees, and in the grass under our feet.

Inside the hop garden at that time of the morning it would be quiet and peaceful, giving me the same feeling I have when I go into the garden at home early in the morning or late evening. I might hear someone at another bin, just the crunch as they picked the bines clean. Soon others would be coming and the brogue of the Londoner, and of the gypsies, mingled with our country talk, all making a picture I shall remember for all time.

The time was long past when we took a billy can to work, and at eleven thirty would make a fire. School holidays then coincided with hop picking. At noon we made our tea. That changed for the Thermos, but the smell of wood smoke brings back memories.

Then came an even newer invention, the hop picking machine. It was of great interest to the town, and visitors came up and watched. T.V. cameras also filmed us, with one other man and our farmer. There were a lot of teething troubles. Rollers got clogged, hops didn't go through, or were not picked cleanly, and once that first year, a bar broke, fortunately missing everyone, or there would have been a casualty. I didn't dislike the work but nothing can replace the hop picking in the garden. There was far more waste too, and our old foreman who attended to the waste end was very put out for he liked every hop picked from the bines, and all hops picked before moving to another set.

We found time to take up outside activities. The children went to Sissinghurst School, and were asked to enter a garden on a plate in the children's section of the flower show. We all went along in the afternoon. It was held in a lovely old house and garden, with various side shows and a fancy dress competition. Gerald had won a third for his garden plate, and this fired us for the future.

The next year Syd entered for the vegetable section, also his sweetpeas – his one love in the flower line. They were started in the Autumn, nursed all winter against frosts, then grown up canes, and when they began blooming had to be picked every day to prevent the pods from forming. I don't know how many carrots Syd didn't dig up to get five of an equal size, but we had a huge garden, and we liked carrots so we could use them up.

The children wanted to go in fancy dress. I had Judy's already, lucky signs all over her dress, very simple, but they seemed to go down well. As for Gerald, I couldn't think what to put him in as he wanted to be a robber and have a

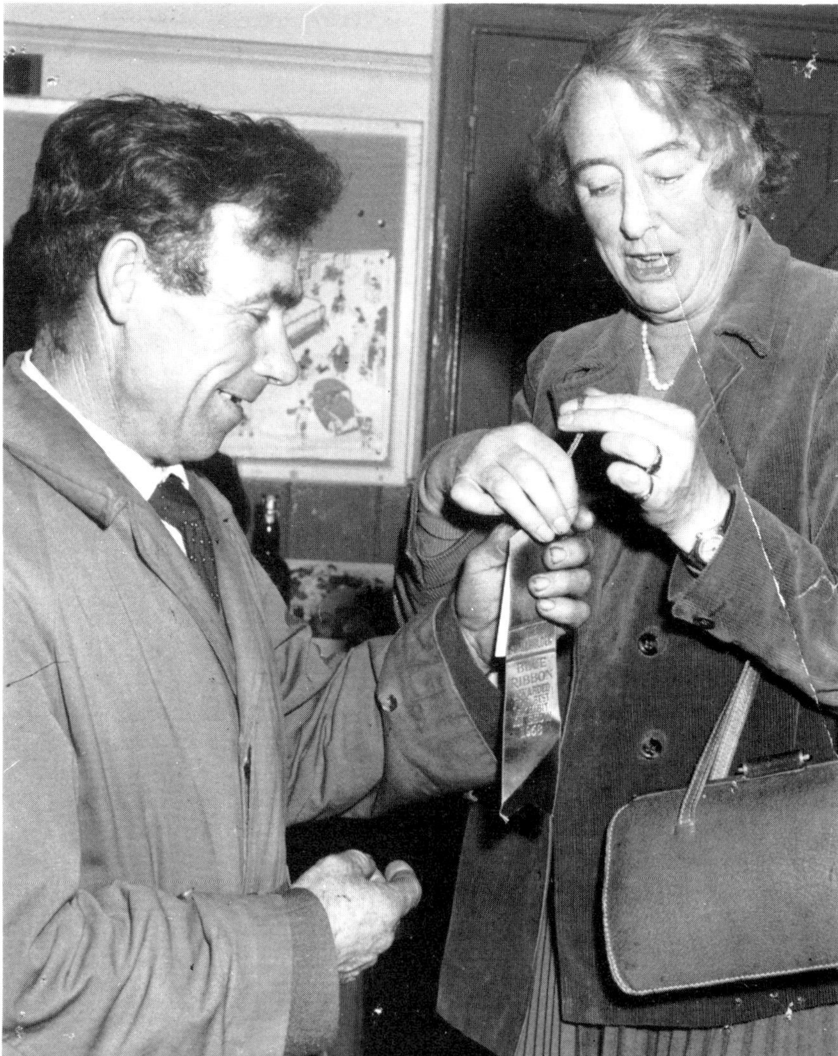

Lady Nicholcon presents the blue ribbon for 'best exhibit in show' by Syd.

Gerald as 'The Sun' at a flower show.

patch over his eye, but pirates were run of the mill, and it was bound to be duplicated. Finally in desperation since he couldn't be left out, I just stuffed his pants out with paper and under his jersey, put a big piece of jam sponge in one hand and a lolly in the other and put him in as a greedy boy. He won first prize, and after that we thought up all sorts of things for them to go as. One year we put Gerald and his friend Terry in as two fishermen. We draped their bodge for the occasion with garden netting, and wrapped a silvery ground sheet we had round Judy's legs. She wore just a flesh coloured swimsuit I happened to have by, we cut out the odd star fish, and with Judy's long fair hair hanging nearly to her waist at that time, we entered the whole in the wheeled section as 'The fish that didn't get away'. That won first prize as well. We started competing in other fêtes as well. Once Gerald went as Mr Cube, his trolley filled with empty sugar packets. They were hard cardboard then, not like the collapsible packs of today. Mr Cube was advertised everywhere at that time. Once again he won.

Syd was doing well in the cottager section of the flower show, and I made jam and bottled fruit. I never made cakes and sponges to come up like other people's so I didn't put any in. I usually came somewhere with my preserves. So we were all contented.

Twice Syd won the Cottagers Cup and also the Banksian Medal. We have a photograph of him being presented with it by Lady Nicolson.

Later on Judy won most points in the cookery section open to all, and won a shield equally with another, but by then she had left the Cranbrook school.

She had won a scholarship to Maidstone Technical College. Her days were very full, since she had to leave home at 7.50 a.m. and didn't arrive back till 6 p.m. Then after the first year she would be doing homework till late on into the evenings, so she had only a few hours to revert to being a tomboy on Saturdays.

Her ambition was to be a vet, or at least to work with animals. Her teacher had persuaded her to think of an alternative, in case she couldn't manage the very difficult subjects needed for a vet. Finally she settled for a catering course, so for a long time we were being fed on different diets. It was at the college that she discovered her ability to paint, not at that time in oils, but her watercolours were very good. I found her studies took up all her time, so I couldn't ask her to help in the house much, except on a Sunday when we went through all the new recipes, so we left her to do the cooking. It was fun, we all took an interest in what she was learning. Later on she went to Caldecott's Community at the weekend, straight from college on Friday. There, she and a friend helped out with the cooking, but carried on with their homework when the children of Caldecott's had theirs, and then came home on a Sunday afternoon. We saw very little of her except at holiday times. It was all swot, school and Caldecott's at the weekends. Then it was time to take her City and Guilds. One of the judges came from St Thomas's hospital and he chose Judy and one other to work at another of the St Thomas's hospitals. It was here that Judy met the boy she was to marry.

I had already joined the Mothers' Union and the W.I., and was on the committee of the Gardeners' Society, so my time was really full. I loved it; no longer did I feel inferior, as Sissinghurst people made me feel one of themselves. I can only liken the village to Ambridge, the radio one, where everyone regardless of class just pulls together to make a go of whatever project is undertaken.

The boundaries were far flung, stretching a long way along the Maidstone Road in one direction, while we at Farningham were at the extreme end on the road to Benenden. So going to these meetings meant a long bike ride or walk. Often one or the other of us would be without a bike, needing new tyres perhaps. In such cases we worked out a quite useful arrangement. If two were going with only one bike, then one would start off cycling and the other would start walking. Then the cyclist would stop so far up the road, prop the bike in a convenient place and start walking, while the other would take the bike on reaching it and ride on past the other one, and so on until we reached our destination. It was surprising how soon we got there, and as we had only walked half the road each it didn't seem so bad.

We had a lovely old vicar in the parish, one in a million. His boast was that he visited everyone in the parish, and I believe he did. If we were working on the farm he seemed to know and would call in the evening, suddenly appearing.

On one particular occasion, I had just brought in my day-old chicks which I was rearing without a broody hen, so at night I popped them in a basket lined with flannel by the kitchen boiler. I had them in ready to cover up a bit so that they didn't escape when in came the vicar. We had our chat, and he asked the children how school was (we had next door's two in as well). We all knelt down to pray before he left. Then some of those chicks got out and were running round the kitchen and one got on to a stool by the vicar as he knelt at the table. Now anyone who knows about the habits of chickens will recognise that a bird will put his head on one side preparing to fly on to a certain place. Well, that chick had designs on the vicar's head as a roosting place. I expected every minute that it would fly. No-one had his eyes shut except the vicar. Then one of my children, I don't know which, gave a snigger, which the others all took up.

That poor man carried on with his prayer, shook hands, said to the children 'See you at Sunday School', and went. What he thought of us, and what he thought it was all about I will never know.

Somehow the Church has always played a part in my life. This particular vicar made sure we all came to church when anyone special was coming. He would send a card to say that he would send a car to pick up from the three cottages, so of course we had to go. He would take the Parish Magazines into 'The Bull' to find one of our cottagers who had a habit of going there on Saturday evenings. He seemed to know all our movements.

I had at last got over my inferiority complex. The people of Sissinghurst were such jolly people, and everyone became involved in one way or another in the two Flower Shows and Fêtes that took place each year. There were two outstanding fund-raising efforts we made in the seventeen years I lived in the Sissinghurst parish.

One was for the Coronation. There was an all-out effort to raise money to make a day that would for ever be remembered by the children. We had a meeting in the Church Parish Hall, and then split up into groups meeting in one or the other's houses to plan what we would do. Ladies got together, W.I., Mothers' Union and so on and one thing planned was a row of pennies which I undertook to supervise.

Fortunately it was a lovely day. I got up there at eight o'clock and starting at 'The King's Head' chalked a line, dividing it into sections, each space large enough for 12 pennies, so 20 spaces filled would be £1 (240d). I was to be relieved at lunchtime, and for an hour in the afternoon while I did a bit of shopping. After that I had nothing to do but be there. The village children came out and spent all day with me, buttonholing everyone who came anywhere near us, even some of the cars as they slowed down to see what was happening, and a coin or two came from them with all the children diving after it. That brought back memories of my childhood, when the 'Bean Feasters' came riding into town. The Bean Feasters were the same as a coach excursion is today, and often the occupants would have stopped at a few pubs and be very merry. They would throw out pennies and sweets to the children as they passed and there would be a mad scramble. It would certainly be frowned on today, and with the amount of traffic on our roads it would be highly dangerous.

The shopkeepers ran out of pennies and had to buy them from us, 2/6d worth at a time which we put down in place of the copper to that amount. One little girl was so fired with ambition to get along to the church with the pennies, that

Gerald as an onion boy.

she kept disappearing only to return from goodness knows where with just another penny. Then we realised she was taking them from the beginning of the row to put on the other end. The poor little lass was very upset when we put them all back again.

At the end of the day, latish in the evening, out came the buckets and we began to fill them up, but I had been standing so long I had a job to stoop. The children trooped with us into the hall; in no way could we keep them out. It had after all been their day, and I bet they enjoyed that part of the Coronation as much as anything.

I cannot remember how much we did make, but whatever it was it was well worth it. Even the men thought it a good effort. They had come along for a count up and they were pleasantly surprised, as I don't think they had expected us to do much. Other groups in the village were doing other things, but this was a ladies' effort, with the children of course.

When the day came it rained, so we had the fancy dress in the hall. Judy went as 'All the fun of the Fair'. I thought it was a good effort, but it didn't appeal to the judges and she came nowhere. I had suggested a dress for a grown up friend of mine – National Emblems – and that won first prize. Gerald won in his class as Mr Cube. Judy promised to lend her dress to a friend, who wore it and took first prize in Cranbrook, so the dress won after all.

A village pantomime at Sissinghurst. Dorothy has the largest moustache.

There could be no doubt as to who was going to win the first prize in our village. It had just been announced that Everest had been climbed by Hillary and Tensing, and one enterprising young lad came dressed in pack and climbing gear 'Just back from the expedition'. It had to be a winner, and was thought up and done in a few minutes.

There was a tea in the hall afterwards. Some things had to be cancelled because of the unreliable weather, but it was a wonderful Coronation (my third), but the most rewarding because I had been involved in the running of it in our village.

This started me taking up various voluntary activities. I had joined a group who ran a World Relief Fund. We raised money to help people suffering from famine or made homeless by wars, earthquakes and so on.

At about that time the Duke of Edinburgh launched the Freedom from Hunger Campaign. I agreed to try and form a committee in Sissinghurst. It was easy to say yes, but I had butterflies when I set out, and it didn't help when at the very first house the little dog came running round the corner and out of the gate I had left open into the street. There was me, plus the owner, plus a few villagers all trying to catch a little dog who was having a whale of a time out there in the road. There wasn't much traffic about fortunately for me. The little dog was finally caught by another man who had been watching all the fun.

It wasn't a very good beginning to my effort, but when I said what I had called about and apologized for not closing the gate behind me I was pleased to hear the lady say that she had every sympathy. As she had a full time job she was not able to join herself, but she would give me a list of names of local people whom she knew were interested. She was sure they would help me, so over a cup of coffee, this she did. It went like a house on fire after that. I had no refusals and our Committee was formed.

We had all the information about the project – what was needed, and where the money could go. It would need £400 to support a whole village comprising about 100 people (mostly one family) for a year, which didn't seem much even by our standards at that time. Items needed were cows or oxen, some farm implements for cultivation, a drill, grain, and enough in the bank to cope with the unexpected disaster such as a typhoon.

We decided to wait and see how we got on before we finally settled what we would give, but at the back of our minds there was always the feeling 'Wouldn't it be nice if we could manage a whole village'.

Meanwhile we drew up a programme of fund raising events, and the result was that we were able to donate enough for the village.

At the end of the Campaign we had a thank you letter from the Duke of Edinburgh.

Chapter 19

THE FAMILY GROWS UP

Judy by now had left Technical College and gone to St Thomas's Hospital as cook. We didn't feel very happy at her going so far away, especially to London, for she at eighteen and a half was still a tomboy country girl.

I needn't have worried, I had an understanding with her that she would let me know if anything was wrong, and she took me at my word. The cook she was under was a tartar, and would pick on anyone who didn't stand up to her, and Judy did not. I had a letter from her every day for the first few weeks, and she came home on her days off. Then I got a letter 'I'm coming home', 'I can't stand it any longer', 'Cook is a Beast', etc etc. Poor Judy, she poured out all troubles just as she would have spoken. I think she is very fortunate to be able to put on paper all she is thinking. Reading her letters is like having her in the room with me. Soon after this particular letter things improved when she was moved to a Nurses' home on Chelsea Embankment. Here she met Tommy. He was a Geordie and was in R.E.M.E. doing his National Service. A few of them were at Chelsea barracks to service the vehicles there. He took Judy around London: it was nice to know that someone was at hand to look after her. He came down to spend a weekend with us and we all liked him on sight. He went back to South Shields after his two years stint was finished. Judy went up to meet his people, and soon they were engaged.

We had our first ever real holiday that year. Jo was settled and had three bonny babies. Judy was in London and shortly to be married. So we booked a bungalow at St Mary's Bay just outside Dymchurch. That holiday was the best because it was the first, the sea was just across the road, and every evening we walked the whole way to the fun fair along the edge of the tide. Coming back the moon would be out and reflected on the water. We all felt better for that holiday.

Judy's wedding was quite different from Joyce's. She decided to have a model gown and thought it would be cheaper to hire it. So, off we went to a place near Oxford Street. I met Judy in London and we went in with a few misgivings. The gowns were shown to us and they were so beautiful that we couldn't imagine that they had ever been used. They were cleaned after each wearing and were only used a few times. There was one really lovely outfit there with nine underskirts, a tiara and veil and even sandals and gloves. Judy fell in love with it, so we dared to ask the price. It was quite as much as buying an ordinary outfit. What Judy intended to pay was just for one day's wear, but well, it had to be that outfit, so Judy paid up and out we came with a large parcel and a slim purse.

It was a lovely wedding. Tom and his brother, who was to be Best Man, came down on the Friday night. Syd had another new suit, and I pressed it and put it

Jo driving the hop-bines to the oasthouse.

safely where I couldn't possibly lose it. But we still had the last minute flap. Does any wedding go off smoothly, I wondered? Joyce's little daughter, Josie, was one of the two bridesmaids and on the day, came up early to get ready with the rest of us. Now, what with the excitement and being away from her mum Josie suddenly burst out crying and didn't want to be a bridesmaid. Poor Judy, she nearly had a fit and so did Syd, but I know all about these last minute fears, so I just said casually 'Oh well, never mind. Judy, you just go and do your nails. Pity about Josie, I've got a lovely little polish for her nails and that lovely pinky rouge to put just a weeny bit on her cheeks.' It wasn't long before Josie sat there and held out her two little hands with the nail varnish on them and yet another crisis was over.

This time we had caterers to do the reception and we hired the village hall. Two unusual things happened. One was the old Geordie custom of scattering coins by the Best Man to all the children watching outside the church, the other thing was the chef's hat which was presented to Judy from St Thomas's main kitchen staff. She had ended her pre-marriage career there and was sorry to be leaving so many friends. That hat was autographed by seventeen chefs.

Gerald was near to leaving school by this time. He had had a lot of ground to make up, for he had lost nearly a year's schooling while he had meningitis. The first full school year afterwards he was trying to keep up with the rest of his class. They had thought it best not to keep him down, but to let him move up with the others, so he did a little homework, and at eleven went to Swattenden, the secondary modern school. Here he began to make strides, going from eighth place at the end of the first term, until when he left he had got to the top, coming first in maths, metalwork and woodwork.

He wanted to be an Electrical Engineer, so when he went to see the Youth Employment Officer that is what he said. She was rather doubtful about his chance of success in that line but suggested that he and his friend should try Chatham Dockyard. If they did pass for engineering then it would mean going to Southampton Docks. As it happens neither of them passed. They were told by letter that though they had reached the required standard there were too many applicants for the places, but they could try again later.

Gerald's headmaster suggested that he stay on at school and start a day release course at Maidstone Technical College. He successfully applied for a job as an Apprentice Electrician with Seeboard at Hawkhurst, going on to pass his H.N.C. in electrical engineering. During this period he wired our house for electricity, and bought a small motor to power it. At last we had a house on a roadside with a bus passing the door, our own electricity when that motor went – usually after a kick – and, finally, Calor gas. It was here we stayed for seventeen years.

Later Gerald had the chance to train as an engineer and started work at Eastbourne. He acquired his own home at Willingdon, but came home at weekends to collect a change of clothes and to raid the larder. At Eastbourne he met Diane, his future wife. They were married at her house in Hartley Wintney, and as it was a long way for us, we hired a minibus to take the family and close friends.

So, after a happy childhood, very different from my own, the last of my brood settled down to married life.

Chapter 20

MY SPECIAL EFFORT

Now that Judy was settled in the North we had somewhere to go, and a marvellous place for a holiday. At first we went up by coach, travelling at night and arriving about 7 a.m. It was jolly cold in the winter, even though the Northern United supplied blankets. Once I took a huge polythene bag, and after the midnight break for tea I got into it and tied it round my waist. It caused a bit of amusement, but who cared – we were always a friendly lot on those coaches.

Judy's husband Tom would hire a car and take us out to some of the places of interest around the north-east coast – Durham, Bamborough Castle, Holy Island and wonderful trips down awe-inspiring passes. It was something new, something to wonder at; our holidays were a real adventure. I realised how little I knew of this country we live in, and determined to see as much as I could of it when and if the chance arrived.

One thing I had noticed in the north-east was how differently they treated their old age pensioners. Shops seemed to have a soft spot for the oldies, giving cheaper meals at certain times in some restaurants. Pensioners could also buy very small portions of food, meat, liver and so on, and an inch or so of cucumber instead of half if they wished. On the buses everyone in South Shields of pensionable age travelled free between 9 a.m. and 4 p.m., and from 6 p.m. onward. All they had to do was show a pass.

I resolved to find out more about why one council gave free travel when another did not, so when I got back home I started asking questions. I was staggered to find that it depended on the council concerned. Quite a lot did give something like 6p off the journey or half-fare, while travel was free in London and Liverpool.

I was now a pensioner myself, and it had always been my maxim that if there was anything that was not right, every effort should be made to put it right, and then, and only then, could one feel free to have a moan about it.

In the part of Kent where I lived there were no bus concessions but in every other part of the county there seemed to be special arrangements. One place had a pensioners' free bus twice a day, while another gave half-fare up to 18p. There could be 6p, 4p, 3p or 2p off journeys depending on the area one lived. The more I studied the subject the more I discovered about what I considered a very unjust state of affairs.

Then I found out that monies paid out in this way came from one's own council, from a Rate Support Grant issued by the Government for use by councils as they wished. Some might spend it on playing fields, others on day centres perhaps. The ways the money could be used were many, and some councils did not consider bus fares for pensioners a special priority. I couldn't see why the Government didn't give a half-fare nationally to all pensioners, thus making sure all had the same treatment. So this was to be my effort – something I had to do before I could really have a good moan at the cost of the bus, which had escalated rapidly over the last few years.

First I collected a lot of paper and headed each sheet with a notice that the people listed below would like the Government to give half-fare nationally to all pensioners and the disabled. I clipped this to a board, took a stock of pens, and set out.

I hadn't any set idea of how to go about it, but I got signatures from all in the bus queue, so decided to do bus queues. I hopped on the bus and got off at Brenchley, joined a queue for a bus going in the opposite direction and just stood there. Everyone was ready to sign, for those who weren't pensioners would be one day, or they knew someone who was. Then another bus came in, and on I went again. At one time on a bus from Tunbridge Wells I didn't even know where I was, but I found the same eagerness to sign. I unclipped a couple of pages and other people stood about and also collected signatures.

I hope I wasn't doing anything illegal. I wasn't accosted anyway so it must have been all right. I was offered lunch with a lady in Southborough, an entire stranger, and had a little rest getting home later in the evening. Buses were not too plentiful on that route, so I dared not leave it later.

Having done this in two or three directions, and collected in all the sheets from the people who were helping, I had to decide what to do with the signatures. Where should I send them? Or should I take them to our local M.P.? Finally I had a talk with a Councillor I knew, not of my parish, but a wonderful person who gave me all the encouragement she could to get this crusade going. It was she who suggested going to Downing Street, and taking my petition myself. She paved the way, asking for permission, stating our time of arrival at No.10, notifying the Police of our coming and so on.

She and I, with an enthusiastic friend from Tunbridge Wells, met in London. Having a few minutes to wait we went to see the Changing of the Guard, then walked round the corner to the famous street. There were a lot of people on the opposite side of the road, including the camera man from our local paper. A policeman stopped me at the little fence arrangement halfway across the road, and asked if I was the 'Lady from Kent'. 'Go along, it's just 11.30' he said. Another officer knocked on the door to say we had arrived, then the door was shut. 'You're to be highly honoured' he said; 'you're to be admitted to present your petition.' A few minutes later the door opened and we were inside. All I could see after the glare outdoors was very dark panelling, another policeman and a few other people. One made himself known to us, explaining that he was the Prime Minister's secretary, and he listened to what we had to say. It was very good, because we felt we had a chance to air a grievance. We told him how unfair the present set-up was, and that it should be a national affair. He promised to let Mr Wilson know all we had said, and agreed to take the petition to him personally. He shook our hands and we were outside again: it had been a great experience.

Dorothy holding her petition on the steps of No.10 Downing Street.

After we had posed for a photo on the steps of No.10 with the policeman standing alongside, an American touched me on the arm. 'Well done' she said. 'Fancy you just going in and talking to your Prime Minister like that, we couldn't do that at the White House'. We didn't enlighten her that we hadn't seen Mr Wilson.

If I had had any idea of what that project of mine was going to lead me into, and where it was going to take me, I don't think I would have ventured on it. I answered every letter in the local paper complaining about higher fares, and went to listen at a public meeting where the Bus Company was applying to raise the fares yet again.

It was held in the Town Hall at Maidstone. We sat down, and I asked an attendant if it was permissible for anyone to get up and ask questions as one does at a Parish Council annual general meeting. I had to write my name and address in a book, and so did my friend. The whole morning was spent in hearing facts and figures, but in the afternoon the Chairman, who sat on a raised platform like a sort of god, looked at his notes and said 'We will hear Mrs Hatcher first'.

To my horror I discovered that I was expected to walk the whole length of the hall between benches filled with business-like men, and sit in a chair below the Chairman. I was terrified. I had no idea I would be given the chance to speak like that, and I wasn't prepared. My legs turned to jelly before I got halfway, but finally I reached the chair and sat down. 'Now Mrs Hatcher' said the Chairman, 'What do you wish to say?' Well, here was my chance. Suddenly all fear left me. I found myself explaining all that I thought was wrong, the everlasting fare rises, and the fact that we had no concessions to ease them. When I had finished he said 'Thank you Mrs Hatcher. Now I want to ask you something. What have you done about it?' 'I asked our Council to do something, and I went to Downing Street with a petition'. As I said that I could *feel* the atmosphere in the room. I gave the Chairman a copy of the letter I had received in response to my petition, saying that the Government was aware of the problem, but left it to the discretion of local councils as to how their money was allocated.

Now I know what it meant to be thrown in at the deep end.

Following the hearing I got in touch with a group who had formed an association to promote a better understanding between those who run the buses and those who use them.

At Cranbrook we were on two bus routes, one from Maidstone to Hastings and one from Tunbridge Wells to Tenterden. We also had a daily coach to London. In the evenings we could find ourselves unable to go places because we couldn't get back. But when I found that many villages had no bus at all, or only one or two a week, I realised how lucky I was compared to some people. Some villagers had no way of reaching a post office if their local one had closed. It wasn't just the fares, or the lack of a subsidy; it was the absence of a bus at all. Some places had no bus after six on Saturday until Monday morning. I had to widen my campaign to take in such things as mothers with young children being unable to get to surgery, or villagers unable to get a prescription because the

Dorothy and Syd on their Golden Wedding Day.

chemist was in a different town. A visit to the dentist might take best part of a day. Many disabled people could not use a bus because they couldn't manage the high steps. All these things could be discussed at our meetings, and we tried to bring the hardships involved to the notice of the authorities.

We did have a measure of success. The Bus Company took notice of what we said, though they also had their problems. They had to break even. They relied on County grants to make up for the losses on little-used routes, but they found it an unequal struggle. Now I could see that buses on those areas should run as a social service.

The County Council issued their Structure Plan for the years ahead, and after reading it through, although I felt I should never understand it all, I was convinced that something must be done to oppose it, especially where it talked about buses in rural areas. I sent off the form, and in due course found that I was to be allowed to go and state why I opposed the plan at the hearing at Maidstone. I wrote out and rewrote my reasons, then tore some up and started again. Eventually I had it all typed.

At Maidstone this time my seat was quite near the people who were hearing what we had to say. I sat down and poured out a glass of water, not realising the microphones were on. There were ice-cubes in that jug of water, and the noise they made plopping into the glass had to be heard to be believed. People all round turned to stare, some giving me a look of commiseration, others obviously thinking 'What can you expect from such an ignoramus?' (My inferiority complex was still not quite dead.) After that I sat as still as a mouse, hardly daring to move, but eventually my turn came. My objections were read, I answered questions quite calmly, and it was over.

I found myself at Southern TV quite out of the blue. A man rang me saying they had been given my name in connection with bus travel in rural areas. Could they come to interview me? This they did later that morning, transporting me by TV van to Hawkhurst depot. There I was put on a 297 bus (the one that serviced my area) and taken for a ride, being interviewed on the way. But the bus didn't go along its normal route. It was quite an adventure as I hadn't dreamed that I was likely to be doing anything of the sort when I got up that morning. It was nice to get an insight into how things operate, and to see the trouble TV staff take to get details for the news they transmit to us on the box. I was glad of the opportunity to see it.

After the hearing of the Structure Plan I took a long look at all that had come up, and wondered whether, or if, anything would come of it. I have come to realise that the result of any understanding will be a gradual process happening over a long period. Progress may be hardly noticeable. Now and again something one has been pressing to achieve for a long time comes to pass quite unobtrusively.

Chapter 21

CHANGES

There is very little left to say except to comment on how things have changed during my lifetime, sometimes for the better, sometimes not. We had a zinc bath to do the washing with the aid of a possum, a sort of bell-like contraption with holes in it on a handle, which one held and banged down on the clothes in the tub. Now, we have a huge variety of soap powders to choose from and a washing machine, which can be switched on and left to get on with it, while the housewife does something else. We made do with a bar of primrose soap bought some weeks earlier, then cut into hand-sized pieces and put away to get hard. This made it go further. We also had a blue bag to aid whitening. Materials were of cotton, linen and artificial silk and all needed careful washing. Woollens could shrink up to a board if washed in too hot water. Cottons needed starching – at least shirts, petticoats and pinnies did. Collars and cuffs needed cold water starch. So Monday was a very busy day, with water to get in from the well, coppers to light, regular feeding to save them from going out, two lots of starch to make and then the drying and damping down of starched clothes before ironing. Oh yes, wash day, old style, is something I'm glad to see the back of. Even those who have no washing machines often use a launderette today and so much is drip dry that the old wash day blues have gone forever.

Cooking too has a new look. No longer do we wrestle with the old kitchen range. How I hated that one I had in service in the farm house I worked at. A more cantankerous sulky black monster never existed. I would rake out all the dead ashes, carefully lay the sticks criss-cross in the bottom of the grate, twiggy birch ones to start with and gradually thicker ones, and finally a layer of small coal, then light the paper and go off to clean the fireplace in the dining room, coming back into the kitchen, not to find a nice glowing layer of red coals ready to receive more coal to burn, oh dear no. Either I would find a blackened mass of half-burned sticks which had gone out or, on a very windy day, the whole lot would have burnt out and disappeared altogether so I had to do it all again. I just had to get up half an hour earlier to make sure I had the fire burning and breakfast cooked by eight o'clock. Then there were the flues. On Friday I arose half an hour earlier still, to do the beastly flues and this is when that range really got its own back for all the nasty names I had been calling it all the week. No sooner had I opened that flue trap into the chimney than out came a huge cloud of soot that billowed out into every corner of the kitchen, meaning more work to do before breakfast. I would gently rake off the tin roof, holding my breath and hoping it would all come out in a nice steady little stream, trying to ease it all onto the paper. I would put layers of paper onto the stove to prevent too much mess. Then, without warning, out would tumble a hard lump of soot blowing all round the room, up my nose, in my eyes, ears and mouth. I had to do two washings of the floor and myself before I could get on with the daily job of the lighting of the grate and boiling the kettle by 7.30 a.m. for the tea, and then cooking breakfast. Then there was the weather to contend with. A windy day meant more scuttles of coal to get in and I would be everlastingly making up the fire. But, on some days, nothing, nothing would get that dratted oven hot enough to bake. Newspapers on the oven door, wood laid over the top of the oven, we tried all ways, but that range was my master and did as it liked.

I wouldn't go back to those days of flues and coal ranges, but they were cheaper even with coal the price it is. That range boiled up to four pots at a time on the top, baked an oven full of food, heated the water and made the most delicious toast I've ever tasted. No toast can come up to it, and all on the one fuel intake. As I said, I don't really want to go back to that time, but if some brainy person could invent a cooker that does all that the range did from one push button, well, that would be the day.

My old hay box, of the dear old Auntie Bea days, does have a modern counterpart in the new up to date slow boiler, which cooks casseroles so beautifully and slowly for no more heat than a single electric bulb. So perhaps somebody is trying to do something to help.

Electric light is certainly something the old life could never offer. Press the switch today and the room is flooded with light – no nasty candles dropping grease all over the place, no messy oil lamps to refill or glasses to replace every time there is a sharp frost. Then quite often when I lit the lamp there would be a ping and a glass would have gone. Once I had four lamp glasses go in one week, but that was during the war years when glass was not so good. I have had glass lamps that lasted for years and years. Then there were the wicks that would work up. I would come back to find the room full of black smudges over everything. The smoke wasn't like that from a fire. It came out in small black particles that seemed to chain themselves together to make a room full of cobwebs. Syd said the cobwebs were already there, but I knew differently.

The village seems to show at a glance the great change in our way of rural life. Gone are the stooks of corn which stood for a full three weeks every harvest time in the fields. So are the haystacks and the tinkling water running in the ditches under the hedges and along the roadside, taking away the surface water. The lengthman, usually a man working for the local council and nearing retirement, would be given the job of looking after a stretch of road, to sweep, to keep the grass verges cut back and edged, to clear the openings into the ditch from the road. We had one who did the road near us, up the hill where the road joined the parish of Benenden, past our house and up to Sissinghurst Street. As soon as he finished he would start all over again. He was known by everyone; the children on their way to school and the housewives on the way to the shops all knew him and stopped to have a chat with our particular lengthman.

Along with the haystacks and stooks of corn we have also lost the thresher. Threshing was an annual event. The corn would be cut, stooked, stacked and

Haymaking as it used to be.

thatched against the day when the thresher could manage to get around to a particular farm. Then all other work would stop on that day of days. Only such essentials as milking, feeding stock and so on had to be done, and all hands and many outsiders were needed to make up the threshing team, and would be pressed into service. I did it at one farm only. My job was to stand on the thresher taking the sheaf from the man on the stack, cutting the bond and passing it to the man actually feeding the thresher. I had to be careful to cut it beside the knot so that a nice piece of useful string was left afterwards for some other purpose. It was hard dusty work, but women got a little extra for helping on that job, so I didn't mind. Besides, I liked doing something different, and there isn't much else to do during the winter months.

I took care to wear dungarees, forerunners of the present day jeans, and wore bicycle clips round the ankles after I had felt a soft movement around my waist one day which turned out to be a mouse. Wellingtons have now replaced galoshes for field work, and they are a great improvement, easy to pull on and take off with no chance of them coming off in the mud as my old galoshes often did.

I well remember my old bike, a 'sit up and beg' type, which I used for many years. I wore out so many tyres on those old rough country lanes that it often meant a few weeks without it, while I saved up enough to get the 4/11d to buy a new one. Then, more likely than not, Joyce would have grown out of her shoes or scuffed the toes so badly that the 4/11d would have to go for new shoes instead. We had no family allowance to save up for such things, nor maternity grant, except for £2.00 which a husband got for each new baby, which went to pay for the nurse. Most of today's mothers are encouraged to have their babies in hospital, and a good thing too, where medical attention is at hand for any emergency.

A school friend of mine died in childbirth just two days after Joyce was born. I was very glad it wasn't before, I would have been really frightened. In spite of all that columnists write in the newspapers about people living below the breadline, it is a joy to see all children nicely dressed, no bare feet or toes hanging out of shoes, no half starved children with pinched faces as I well remember. Thank God mine never did get to that stage. We had to struggle to make ends meet but we managed. We did make clothes more then than we do now. Gerald's little buster suits were often made from the best parts of his dad's shirts, decorated with stripes of blue material or even prints or anything I could lay my hands on. Neither did we make so much use of the easy payment clubs in existence today. One did not dare saddle the housekeeping with what we were not sure of being able to meet, so we made do. If my shoes were too run down then I didn't go out until I could afford to have them mended. The round screw-on rubber heel pads were a boon, and could be twisted round for even wear. I often had to fill a hole in my shoe by putting in a piece of lino if I couldn't afford to have them repaired.

The coming of the hop machines made the largest difference to our way of life. It was a wonderful invention, doing the work of many men and women, but very wasteful. It was said that many more hops had to be grown to make up for the wastage. There were hops strewed about on the ground in the hop fields where the bines were pulled down. In the old days of hand hop picking, every hop had to be gathered up before we could pick up our bin and take it to a new part of the hop garden. Everything seemed to change overnight with the coming of the machine. It stood in a low open sided shed with huge hooks on an iron chain on which the bines were hung. These went down into the pickers, and first some of the branches were knocked off, then further on pluckers would knock off more hops. The bines continued on their way and the hops were carried on to a conveyor belt to the end where people stood and removed any leaves which the fan hadn't sucked off. Thank goodness I didn't have to go on picking out the leaves — I really would have gone up the wall. It was just one long boring sameness. I wouldn't work in a factory for anything. My job was to strip off any branches that remained on the bines before they were sawn automatically into pieces to be rotted down for manure.

Soon all farms seemed to be mechanised and could be run on a handful of men instead of the staff of earlier days. I liked working in the hop machine shed, but much preferred the hop garden where so many different sounds could be heard as one sat on the corner of the bin picking away at the hops, only stopping at the cry of the measurer 'get your hops ready'. What a scramble that was. I never could pick out the leaves as I went, so there was always a mad rush to get

'When the hop-picking machine broke down we went back to hand-picking'.

An old hayrake still in good condition.

it done when I heard him coming. We had gypsies, Londoners, local people from the towns and the farm women and children. I loved hop picking and it is one of the things I will always look back on with nostalgia. We could tell the time by the wood smoke when the fires were lit and the billy cans put on ready for dinner. The pole puller would put two pieces of wood in the ground, making a rest for the pole on which he would put our billy cans to boil. Later, these went out of fashion when the thermos flasks replaced billy cans, but the tea never tasted the same.

I do wish that perhaps we could keep just one farm for tourists and others to see how we used to live. I did see a collection of farm implements, ploughs, shims, waggons and so on all drawn up on the side of the field at a show, things Syd used to use day in day out during his farmwork. It seems that in just one lifetime we have lost so much that was nice, like the old layered hedge that we used to call Kent hedge, but no doubt it was called something else in different parts of the country. The Kent hedge was quite an art, and the hedger and ditcher took a great pride in 'layering' a hedge. He would cut the bough through nearly to the skin, lay it out, knock in a few stakes, and tie the bough back in. The new shoots would grow upwards, and the result was a nice tidy hedge which was thick and only needed trimming each year.

Now there is a horrible hedge cutter thing that nibbles along the top leaving a gap where there is a pole or tree in it, nothing beautiful about it. To go in for

A cottage at Smallhythe today.

efficiency we lose so much beauty that helped to make the countryside something worth seeing. Even our country walks are restricted by wire fences each side of a narrow path. One cannot blame farmers, as people do not seem to have any concern for the countryside, leaving gates open and breaking down fences. Apple pinching has been done by all small children, but then it was just an apple, while nowadays it is boxes that are stolen from an orchard. So we lose by the curtailment of the rural pleasures once enjoyed on a walk through the countryside.

There have been changes in attitude too.

One good thing is the different outlook of people towards illegitimate children. They are no longer looked down upon beyond a raised eyebrow when someone hears that so and so's girl has got herself pregnant. Even the term is now a little more sophisticated. A girl used to have got herself 'in trouble' and was looked down upon by all, her parents included, who often turned the poor girl out. Now there are people to consult with advice to give, social security if the girl wishes to keep the child, adoption arranged if she finds it best to relinquish it. This is a great step forward, but what has happened to today's morals? In nearly every estate someone is living with someone else's husband or wife, children and wives are left overnight for some other gay young thing, and girls are 'on the pill'. Perhaps it is better than unwanted babies, but doesn't it condone promiscuous behaviour? I was certainly terrified even to talk to a boy because of what might happen if I became too friendly. I once helped down at a Youth Club and a young girl, still at school, went to pay me for her coffee when out of her purse fell a contraceptive. Without any show of embarrassment she just casually picked it up and put it back in her purse. I knew the girl and was rather shocked. Not so my helper. 'Oh well, that's better than an unwanted baby' she said. Another change in the pattern and outlook of our life. It seems to gain something on the one side and lose something on the other.

But, with all the improvements and all the changes for everyone, something somewhere has gone wrong. People seem to want more and more. Because young people have everything at such an early age, there is so much discontent and vandalism in life everywhere, windows of empty houses broken for instance; it just doesn't make sense. There can't be much fun in just breaking a thing for the sheer joy of it, because by the time it's discovered, the culprits will be gone, so they don't even get any fun watching the effect it has on the owner.

But another positive change has been in the provision for old people. Many of the old workhouses have been replaced by council-run homes, with good food, pleasant surroundings and helpers who have time to stop and chat or read letters. Where the old buildings are still in use the stone corridors are camouflaged, there are easy chairs instead of the old wooden benches, and nicely laid out gardens replace the yards. Above all those residents who are able can go out through unlocked doors to the local village or town, to attend 'do's' or visit friends. For those older people unfortunate enough to need help, and who have no relatives able or willing to care for them, the present-day homes provide a comfortable refuge rather than a dismal prison.

How different it is too for a child in care today with a housemother to help them feel part of a family. They have a say in what they wear, and go about just as other children do. It has taken fifty years for these changes to occur, and a lot remains to be done, but the old workhouse and the children's home of yesterday must never return. It has taken too long to build away from them.

Now, with my children all happily settled in homes of their own, I live in a comfortable council flat. But in spite of all its modern conveniences there are times when I miss the countryside – the bird song, the cock crowing, the lowing of cattle. It appears we can't have everything.

Meresborough Books

17 Station Road, Rainham, Gillingham, Kent. ME8 7RS
Medway (0634) 388812

We are a specialist publisher of books about Kent. Our books are available in most bookshops in the county, including our own at this address. Alternatively you may order direct, adding 10% for post (minimum 20p, orders over £20.00 post free). ISBN prefix 0 905270 for 3 figure numbers, 094819 for 4 figure numbers. Titles in print August 1988.

BYGONE KENT. A monthly journal on all aspects of Kent history founded October 1979. £1.20 per month. Annual Subscription £13.00. All back numbers available.

HARDBACKS

THE GILLS by Tony Conway. ISBN 266. £5.95. **BARGAIN OFFER £1.95.**

JUST OFF THE SWALE by Don Sattin. ISBN 045. £5.95.

KENT CASTLES by John Guy. ISBN 150. £7.50.

KENT'S OWN by Robin J. Brooks. The history of 500 (County of Kent) Squadron of the R.A.A.F. ISBN 541. £5.95.

LIFE AND TIMES OF THE EAST KENT CRITIC by Derrick Molock. ISBN 3077. **BARGAIN OFFER £1.95.**

THE LONDON, CHATHAM & DOVER RAILWAY by Adrian Gray. ISBN 886. £7.95.

THE NATURAL HISTORY OF ROMNEY MARSH by Dr F.M. Firth, M.A., Ph.D. ISBN 789. £6.95.

A NEW DICTIONARY OF KENT DIALECT by Alan Major. ISBN 274. £7.50.

O FAMOUS KENT by Eric Swain. ISBN 738. £9.95. **BARGAIN OFFER £4.95.**

THE PAST GLORY OF MILTON CREEK by Alan Cordell and Leslie Williams. ISBN 3042. £9.95.

THE PLACE NAMES OF KENT by Judith Glover. A comprehensive reference work. ISBN 614. **BARGAIN OFFER £4.95.**

ROCHESTER FROM OLD PHOTOGRAPHS compiled by the City of Rochester Society. Large format. ISBN 975. £7.95. (Also available in paperback ISBN 983. £4.95.)

SHERLOCK HOLMES AND THE KENT RAILWAYS by Kelvin Jones. ISBN 3255. £8.95.

SOUTH EAST BRITAIN: ETERNAL BATTLEGROUND by Gregory Blaxland. A military history. ISBN 444. £5.95.

STRATFORD HOUSE SCHOOL 1912-1987 by Susan Pittman. ISBN 3212. £10.00.

TALES OF VICTORIAN HEADCORN or The Oddities of Heddington by Penelope Rivers (Ellen M. Poole). ISBN 3050. £8.95. (Also available in paperback ISBN 3069. £3.95.)

TEYNHAM MANOR AND HUNDRED (798-1935) by Elizabeth Selby, MBE. ISBN 630. £5.95.

TWO HALVES OF A LIFE by Doctor Kary Pole. ISBN 509. £5.95.

US BARGEMEN by A.S. Bennett. ISBN 207. £6.95.

A VIEW OF CHRIST'S COLLEGE, BLACKHEATH by A.E.O. Crombie, B.A. ISBN 223. £6.95.

LARGE FORMAT PICTORIAL PAPERBACKS

ARE YOU BEING SERVED, MADAM? by Molly Proctor. ISBN 3174. £3.50.
AVIATION IN KENT by Robin J. Brooks. ISBN 681. £2.95.
EAST KENT FROM THE AIR by John Guy. ISBN 3158. £3.50.
EAST SUSSEX RAILWAYS IN OLD POSTCARDS by Kevin Robertson. ISBN 3220. £3.50.
EXPLORING OLD ROCHESTER by John Bryant. ISBN 827. £2.95.
FIVE MEDWAY VILLAGES by Wyn Bergess and Stephen Sage. ISBN 649. £2.95.
GEORGE BARGEBRICK Esq. by Richard-Hugh Perks. ISBN 479. £4.50.
GOUDHURST: A Pictorial History by John T. Wilson, M.A. ISBN 3026. £2.95.
KENT TOWN CRAFTS by Richard Filmer. ISBN 584. £2.95.
KENT TRANSPORT IN OLD POSTCARDS by Eric Baldock. ISBN 320. £2.95.
THE LIFE AND ART OF ONE MAN by Dudley Pout. ISBN 525. £2.95.
MORE PICTURES OF RAINHAM by Barbara Mackay Miller. ISBN 3298. £3.50.
THE MOTOR BUS SERVICES OF KENT AND EAST SUSSEX — A brief history by Eric Baldock. ISBN 959. £4.95.
OLD BROADSTAIRS by Michael David Mirams. ISBN 3115. £3.50.
OLD CHATHAM: A THIRD PICTURE BOOK by Philip MacDougall. ISBN 3190. £3.50.
OLD GILLINGHAM by Philip MacDougall. ISBN 3328. £3.50.
OLD HEADCORN by the Headcorn Local History Society. ISBN 3271. £3.50.
OLD MAIDSTONE'S PUBLIC HOUSES by Irene Hales. ISBN 533. £2.95.
OLD MAIDSTONE Vol.1 by Irene Hales. ISBN 096. £3.50.
OLD MAIDSTONE Vol.2 by Irene Hales. ISBN 38X. £2.50.
OLD MAIDSTONE Vol.3 by Irene Hales. ISBN 3336. £3.50.
OLD MARGATE by Michael David Mirams. ISBN 851. £3.50.
OLD PUBS OF TUNBRIDGE WELLS & DISTRICT by Keith Hetherington and Alun Griffiths. ISBN 300X. £3.50.
OLD SANDWICH by Julian Arnold and Andrew Aubertin. ISBN 673. £2.95.
OLD TONBRIDGE by Don Skinner. ISBN 398. £2.50.
PEMBURY IN THE PAST by Mary Standen. ISBN 916. £2.95.
A PICTORIAL STUDY OF ALKHAM PARISH by Susan Lees and Roy Humphreys. ISBN 3034. £2.95.
A PICTORIAL STUDY OF HAWKINGE PARISH by Roy Humphreys. ISBN 328X. £3.50.
A PICTUREBOOK OF OLD RAINHAM by Barbara Mackay Miller. ISBN 606. £3.50.
A PICTUREBOOK OF OLD SHEPPEY by Michael Thomas. ISBN 657. £2.95.
REMINISCENCES OF OLD CRANBROOK by Joe Woodwock. ISBN 331X. £3.50.
ROCHESTER FROM OLD PHOTOGRAPHS — see under hardbacks.
THOMAS SIDNEY COOPER OF CANTERBURY by Brian Stewart. ISBN 762. £2.95.
WEST KENT FROM THE AIR by John Guy. ISBN 3166. £3.50.

STANDARD SIZE PAPERBACKS

BIRDS OF KENT: A Review of their Status and Distribution by the Kent Ornithological Society. ISBN 800. £6.95.

BIRDWATCHING IN KENT by Don Taylor. ISBN 932. £4.50.

THE CHATHAM DOCKYARD STORY by Philip MacDougall. ISBN 3301. £6.95.

CHIDDINGSTONE — AN HISTORICAL EXPLORATION by Jill Newton. ISBN 940. £1.95.

A CHRONOLOGY OF ROCHESTER by Brenda Purle. ISBN 851. £1.50.

COBHAM. Published for Cobham Parish Council. ISBN 3123. £1.00.

CRIME AND CRIMINALS IN VICTORIAN KENT by Adrian Gray. ISBN 967. £3.95.

CURIOUS KENT by John Vigar. ISBN 878. £1.95.

CYCLE TOURS OF KENT by John Guy. No. 1: Medway, Gravesend, Sittingbourne and Sheppey. ISBN 517. £1.50.

DOVER REMEMBERED by Jessie Elizabeth Vine. ISBN 819. £3.95.

EXPLORING KENT CHURCHES by John E. Vigar. ISBN 3018. £3.95.

EXPLORING SUSSEX CHURCHES by John E. Vigar. ISBN 3093. £3.95.

FLIGHT IN KENT. ISBN 3085. £1.95.

FROM MOTHS TO MERLINS: The History of West Malling Airfield by Robin J. Brooks. ISBN 3239. £4.95.

THE GHOSTS OF KENT by Peter Underwood. ISBN 86X. £3.95.

A HISTORY OF CHATHAM GRAMMAR SCHOOL FOR GIRLS, 1907-1982 by Audrey Perkyns. ISBN 576. £1.95.

KENT AIRFIELDS IN THE BATTLE OF BRITAIN by the Kent Aviation Historical Research Society. ISBN 3247. £4.95.

KENT COUNTRY CHURCHES by James Antony Syms. ISBN 3131. £4.50.

KENT COUNTRY CHURCHES CONTINUED by James Antony Syms. ISBN 314X. £5.95.

KENT INNS AND SIGNS by Michael David Mirams. ISBN 3182. £3.95.

LET'S EXPLORE THE RIVER DARENT by Frederick Wood. ISBN 770. £1.95.

LULLINGSTONE PARK: THE EVOLUTION OF A MEDIAEVAL DEER PARK by Susan Pittman. ISBN 703. £3.95.

PENINSULA ROUND (The Hoo Peninsula) by Des Worsdale. ISBN 568. £1.50.

REAL ALE PUBS IN KENT by CAMRA in Kent. ISBN 3263. £1.95.

SAINT ANDREW'S CHURCH, DEAL by Gregory Holyoake. ISBN 835. 95p.

SHORNE: The History of a Kentish Village by A.F. Allen. ISBN 3204. £4.95.

SIR GARRARD TYRWHITT-DRAKE AND THE COBTREE ESTATE, MAIDSTONE by Elizabeth Melling B.A. ISBN 3344. £1.50.

SITTINGBOURNE & KEMSLEY LIGHT RAILWAY STOCKBOOK AND GUIDE. ISBN 843. 95p.

STOUR VALLEY WALKS from Canterbury to Sandwich by Christopher Donaldson. ISBN 991. £1.95.

TALES OF VICTORIAN HEADCORN — see under hardbacks.

WADHURST: Town of the High Weald by Alan Savidge and Oliver Mason. ISBN 3352. £5.95.